ESSENTIALS OF
FORENSIC SCIENCE

Drugs, Poisons, and Chemistry

ESSENTIALS OF
FORENSIC SCIENCE

Drugs, Poisons, and Chemistry

Suzanne Bell, Ph.D.

SET EDITOR
Suzanne Bell, Ph.D.

Facts On File
An imprint of Infobase Publishing

DRUGS, POISONS, AND CHEMISTRY

Facts On File, Inc.
An imprint of Infobase Publishing
132 West 31st Street
New York NY 10001

Library of Congress Cataloging-in-Publication Data

Bell, Suzanne.
    Drugs, poisons, and chemistry / Suzanne Bell.
      p. cm.—(Essentials of forensic science)
    Includes bibliographical references and index.
    ISBN-13: 978-0-8160-5510-4
    ISBN-10: 0-8160-5510-6
    1. Chemistry, Forensic. I. Title.
    RA1057.B46 2009
    615.9—dc22   2008000687

Facts On File books are available at special discounts when purchased in bulk quantities for businesses, associations, institutions, or sales promotions. Please call our Special Sales Department in New York at (212) 967-8800 or (800) 322-8755.

You can find Facts On File on the World Wide Web at http://www.factsonfile.com

Text design by Erik Lindstrom
Illustrations by Dale Williams
Photo research by Suzanne M. Tibor, Ph.D.

Printed in the United States of America

MP ML 10 9 8 7 6 5 4 3 2 1

This book is printed on acid-free paper.

This book is dedicated to the hundreds of forensic chemists working in local, state, federal, and international forensic science laboratories. Their important work is often overshadowed by more glamorous forensic fields, but it is just as critical to ensuring that justice is served.

CONTENTS

PREFACE

Forensic science has become in the early 21st century what the space race was in the 1960s—an accessible and inspiring window into the world of science. The surge in popularity that began in the latter part of the 20th century echoes a boom that began in the later part of the 19th century and was labeled the "Sherlock Holmes effect." Today it is called the "C.S.I. effect," but the consequences are the same as they were a century ago. The public has developed a seemingly insatiable appetite for anything forensic, be it fiction, reality, or somewhere between.

Essentials of Forensic Science is a set that is written in response to this thirst for knowledge and information. Written by eminent forensic scientists, the books cover the critical core of forensic science from its earliest inception to the modern laboratory and courtroom.

Forensic science is broadly defined as the application of science to legal matters, be they criminal cases or civil lawsuits. The history of the law dates back to the earliest civilizations, such as the Sumerians and the Egyptians, starting around 5000 B.C.E. The roots of science are older than civilization. Early humans understood how to make tools, how to cook food, how to distinguish between edible and inedible plants, and how to make rudimentary paints. This knowledge was technical and not based on any underlying unifying principles. The core of these behaviors is the drive to learn, which as a survival strategy was invaluable. Humans learned to cope with different environments and conditions, allowing adaptation when other organisms could not. Ironically, the information encoded in human DNA gives us the ability to analyze, classify, and type it.

Science as a formalized system of thinking can be traced to the ancient Greeks, who were the first to impose systematic patterns of thought and analysis to observations. This occurred around 500 B.C.E. The Greeks organized ideas about the natural world and were able to conceive of advanced concepts. They postulated the atom (from the

Greek word *atomos*) as the fundamental unit of all matter. The Greeks were also among the first to study anatomy, medicine, and physiology in a systematic way and to leave extensive written records of their work. They also formalized the concept of the autopsy.

From ancient roots to modern practice the history of forensic science winds through the Middle Ages, alchemy, and the fear of poisoning. In 1840 pivotal scientific testimony was given by Mathieu-Joseph-Bonaventure (Mateu Josep Bonaventura) Orfila (1787–1853) in a trial in Paris related to a suspected case of arsenic poisoning. His scientific technique and testimony marks the beginning of modern forensic science. Today the field is divided into specialties such as biology (DNA analysis), chemistry, firearms and tool marks, questioned documents, toxicology, and pathology. This division is less than a half-century old. In Orfila's time the first to practice forensic science were doctors, chemists, lawyers, investigators, biologists, and microscopists with other skills and interests that happened to be of use to the legal system. Their testimony was and remains opinion testimony, something the legal system was slow to embrace. Early courts trusted swearing by oath—better still if oaths of others supported it. Eyewitnesses were also valued, even if their motives were less than honorable. Only in the last century has the scientific expert been integrated into the legal arena with a meaningful role. Essentials of Forensic Science is a distillation of the short history and current status of modern forensic science.

The set is divided into seven volumes:

- ☑ *Science versus Crime* by Max Houck, director of research — forensic science, West Virginia University; Fellow, American Academy of Forensic Sciences; formerly of the FBI (trace evidence analyst/anthropologist), working at the Pentagon and Waco. This book covers the important cases and procedures that govern scientific evidence, the roles of testimony and admissibility hearings, and how the law and scientific evidence intersect in a courtroom.

- ☑ *Blood, Bugs, and Plants* by Dr. R. E. Gaensslen, professor, forensic science; head of program and director of graduate studies; Distinguished Fellow, American Academy of Forensic

Sciences; former editor of the *Journal of Forensic Sciences*. This book delves into the many facets of forensic biology. Topics include a historical review of forensic serology (ABO blood groups), DNA typing, forensic entomology, forensic ecology, and forensic botany.

☑ *Drugs, Poisons, and Chemistry* by Dr. Suzanne Bell, Bennett Department of Chemistry, West Virginia University; Fellow of the American Board of Criminalistics; and Fellow of the American Academy of Forensics. This book covers topics in forensic chemistry, including an overview of drugs and poisons, both as physical evidence and obtained as substances in the human body. Also included is a history of poisoning and toxicology.

☑ *Trace Evidence* by Max Houck. This book examines the common types of microscopic techniques used in forensic science, including scanning electron microscopy and analysis of microscopic evidence, such as dust, building materials, and other types of trace evidence.

☑ *Firearms and Fingerprints* by Edward Hueske, University of North Texas; supervising criminalist, Department of Public Safety of Arizona, 1983–96 (retired); Fellow, American Academy of Forensic Sciences; emeritus member of American Society of Crime Laboratory Directors (ASCLD). This book focuses on how firearms work, how impressions are created on bullets and casings, microscopic examination and comparison, and gunshot residue. The examination of other impression evidence, such as tire and shoe prints and fingerprints, is also included.

☑ *Crashes and Collapses* by Dr. Tom Bohan, J. D.; Diplomate, International Institute of Forensic Engineering Sciences; Founders Award recipient of the Engineering Sciences Section, American Academy of Forensic Sciences. This book covers forensic engineering and the investigation of accidents such as building and bridge collapses; accident reconstruction, and transportation disasters.

☑ *Fakes and Forgeries* by Dr. Suzanne Bell. This book provides an overview of questioned documents, identification of hand-writing, counterfeiting, famous forgeries of art, and historical hoaxes.

Each volume begins with an overview of the subject, followed by a discussion of the history of the field and mention of the pioneers. Since the early forensic scientists were often active in several areas, the same names will appear in more than one volume. A section on the scientific principles and tools summarizes how forensic scientists working in that field acquire and apply their knowledge. With that foundation in place the forensic application of those principles is described to include important cases and the projected future in that area.

Finally, it is important to note that the volumes and the set as a whole are not meant to serve as a comprehensive textbook on the subject. Rather, the set is meant as a "pocket reference" best used for obtaining an overview of a particular subject while providing a list of resources for those needing or wanting more. The content is directed toward nonscientists, students, and members of the public who have been caught up in the current popularity of forensic science and want to move past fiction into forensic reality.

ACKNOWLEDGMENTS

I would like to acknowledge the efforts of my coauthors in this set for their work and Ms. Suzanne M. Tibor for her assistance in obtaining many of the great photographs for this and the other volumes.

INTRODUCTION

Chemistry has been described as the central science because many other sciences arise from its principles. Biology is the study of life, and life is the result of complex chemical actions, reactions, and interactions. The scientific bridges linking chemistry and biology are biochemistry and molecular biology. These disciplines seek to understand how chemistry creates life and how life works at the level of chemical reactions. DNA (deoxyribonucleic acid), the molecule that carries genes and directs life, is a chemical compound. Because of its unique chemistry, DNA can self-replicate and control the production of cell proteins. In a modern forensic laboratory DNA typing is one of the principal tools used to study biological evidence.

Like all modern disciplines, chemistry has many subdisciplines and branches. Biochemistry is one, as are organic chemistry, inorganic chemistry, physical chemistry, and analytical chemistry, to name just a few. The American Chemical Society (ACS), the largest scientific society in the world, has more than 160,000 members, 19,000 of which are international and represent more than 100 countries. The ACS (available on the World Wide Web at www.chemistry.org) publishes 36 journals and has nearly 200 local chapters and 33 technical divisions.

The first people to practice what would become chemistry were ancient physicians and pharmacists. They worked mostly with plants and devised teas, extracts, and other materials used to treat illness and injury. Their knowledge came from trial and error and was passed along by apprenticeship. By the time of the ancient Greeks the study of metallurgy had become important because of the value assigned to gold. If gold was to be fairly valued, the ancients realized, they needed a way to measure the purity of gold. Chemists were called on to analyze ores and coins to determine if gold was present, and if so, how much. This need led to the birth of analytical chemistry.

Chemistry and forensic chemistry developed largely from ancient knowledge and techniques associated with medicines. This 4,000-year-old Sumerian clay tablet in the Museum of the University of Pennsylvania has been translated by Dr. Samuel Noah Kramer of the museum and by Dr. Martin Levey of Pennsylvania State College. The tablet contains the oldest-known medical handbook. A portion reads: "White pear tree, the flower of the 'moon' plant, grind into a powder, dissolve in beer, let the man drink." *(Bettmann/CORBIS/ photo dated September 27, 1953)*

Analytical chemists investigate samples to understand their chemical content. This involves two tasks. First, the chemist must determine which chemicals are present, a process called qualitative analysis. A forensic toxicologist will test blood or urine to see what drugs or poisons might be present, while a forensic chemist working in a crime lab would first test a powder to determine what types of illegal drugs are present. The second step is quantitative analysis in which the amount or concentration of individual components is determined. Prior to the development of modern instrumentation, the painstaking process of analyzing a sample started with qualitative analysis, followed by a separate quantitative analysis of each of the components of interest. Often, accurate quantitative analysis was difficult or impossible. In modern forensic chemistry both steps can be accomplished at the same time, although multiple tests are used to ensure that the analysis is correct.

The application of chemistry to sample analysis is central to forensic chemistry. When a white powder is submitted to the lab, the question is always some form of "What is this?" and "How much is present?"

FORENSIC CHEMISTS

Forensic chemists are principally analytical chemists who apply their knowledge and expertise to samples linked to law enforcement or the legal system. Two divisions can be drawn within forensic chemistry. Those who analyze physical evidence such as powders, plant materials, and arson debris are usually referred to as forensic chemists, and they typically work in local, state, or federal crime laboratories. Forensic toxicologists work with drugs, poisons, and their biological by-products in blood and bodily fluids. They are employed in crime labs, medical examiners' offices, and a variety of other places. Other forensic chemists can be found working with trace and biological evidence, but their numbers are smaller.

Required education to enter the field of forensic chemistry includes extensive coursework in chemistry and biology. To work in local, state, or federal crime labs the entry-level education required is usually a bachelor of science degree (B.S.) in chemistry or a closely related natural science such as biology. Specific chemistry courses are required, such as introductory, organic, and analytical chemistry along with substantial laboratory work. Within a few years this minimum may increase to a master's of science degree (M.S.). For entry-level toxicology work, such as alcohol and drug screening, the requirements stress biochemistry and

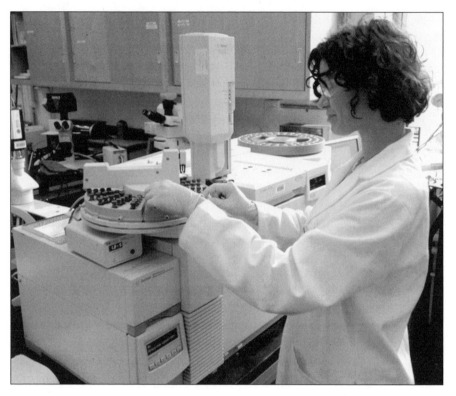

A forensic chemist working with instrumentation in a forensic chemistry laboratory (*Courtesy of the author*)

related subjects. Many toxicologists have a Ph.D. in toxicology or pharmaceutical science.

Both forensic chemists and toxicologists work with drugs and poisons, but each starts with different evidence. A forensic chemist working in a crime laboratory would receive evidence such as plant material suspected of being marijuana or a white powder suspected of being cocaine. These samples are referred to as physical evidence. The chemist would use chemical tests to determine if the evidence is or contains an illegal drug. He or she would also be responsible for samples obtained from suspected arson crimes and might be called upon whenever samples come into the lab that would benefit from chemical analysis. Examples of this type of evidence include materials such as fire debris, soil, paint, glass, explosives, and fibers.

Toxicologists, on the other hand, work with biological evidence such as blood, saliva, urine, and feces. For example, when a person smokes the drug cocaine, that person's metabolism converts the cocaine to other substances that can be found in body fluids such as blood or urine. The toxicologist uses analytical chemistry to identify chemical traces and unmetabolized drugs. Toxicologists often work in labs associated with a medical examiner's (ME) office or a hospital. Unlike forensic chemists, forensic toxicologists usually do not deal with the drug or poison itself but rather biological samples that may contain it or its characteristic breakdown products. They follow the biological trail of a substance once it is ingested.

The field of forensic toxicology can be further broken down into more specific areas. The principal source of casework is usually blood alcohol determinations, in which toxicologists determine the percentage of ethanol present in a blood sample. These samples come from people suspected of drunk driving or related offenses and are often categorized as human performance toxicology. Forensic toxicologists also analyze samples taken as part of employment screening, both for governments and for private companies. Another branch of forensic toxicology is postmortem toxicology, where samples of blood and body fluids are obtained at autopsy.

Toxicologists can be involved in performance toxicology related to sporting events. At the Olympics a sophisticated laboratory is stationed close to the site to analyze samples taken from athletes to ensure that they are not taking banned substances. Many substances that are banned by sporting agencies are not illegal. Athletes are prohibited from taking them because they afford an unfair advantage over other competitors. For example, some antihistamines are banned in sports even though they are not illegal drugs. Sports samples are categorized as human performance toxicology, along with alcohol analysis. All of these substances (alcohol to steroids) affect performance, either by improving or by impairing it.

WHAT IS IN THIS BOOK

Drugs, Poisons, and Chemistry will touch on all aspects of what forensic chemistry was, how it developed, and what it includes today. The first chapter sets the stage through a short history of forensic chemistry: It begins with ancient physicians and pharmacists and moves quickly into the world of poisons. The most famous of these is arsenic. For thousands of years poisoning was the most feared of crimes and arsenic the most famous of poisons. More than any other substance this dull gray metal and its various forms gave birth to forensic chemistry and forensic science. The first chapter tells the story of arsenic and those who developed effective tests to detect it.

The second chapter delves into the tools and techniques used by forensic chemists. Some of these tools are familiar, such as the microscope, while others are less well known, such as the use of antibodies to detect toxins. One of the most important concepts in forensic chemistry is the study of color; this chapter will cover why color is important and how a forensic scientist uses and studies it. The following chapters cover the main areas of forensic chemistry: drug analysis and toxicology. The final chapter examines the state of forensic chemistry today and the trends that appear to be dictating its future. However, to understand where forensic chemistry is going, the place to start is where it began.

History and Pioneers

The history of forensic chemistry winds through the history of analytical chemistry, chemistry, and medicine. The ancient practices and beliefs of alchemy formed the basis of what would become the discipline of chemistry, from which forensic chemistry arose. Alchemy is often categorized as a diversion from science, but alchemy was science for more than a millennium. Alchemists such as Paracelsus, Robert Boyle, and Sir Isaac Newton made discoveries and developed techniques still used in forensic laboratories. Alchemy was the earliest form of analytical chemistry, which is the separation of compounds and elements from each other and from the matrix they are found in. For example, to determine the purity of gold it is necessary to analyze for the gold in a sample; to analyze for gold it is necessary to isolate the gold from any contaminants or adulterants found in it.

Most ancient cultures that left records practiced alchemy, which grew out of mining, metallurgy, and medicine. The undercurrent, even though the ancients did not recognize it, was chemistry. Alchemy was an odd and interesting blend of science, art, and religion that focused on the concept of purification and of separating material that was considered "pure," such as gold, from the impure or whatever it was embedded in. Today's analytical chemist would call the gold the analyte and what it is embedded in the matrix. A forensic toxicologist testing urine for alcohol would call the urine the matrix and the alcohol the analyte. Analytical chemistry depends on the ability to isolate one or more components from a matrix.

The first mentions of alchemy date to around 400 B.C.E. The Greeks had the word *chyma* to describe processes of metalworking, and this might be one origin of *alchemy*, but the Chinese and Egyptians recorded similar words also related to metallurgy. All three cultures practiced alchemy, and the *al* part of the word appears to have come from Arabic,

Paracelsus: A Grandfather of Forensic Toxicology

Paracelsus (1493–1541) was a colorful eccentric, alchemist, philosopher, and writer with unconventional ideas and enormous experimental skills. He was born into a Swiss family and named Philipus Aureolus Theophrastus Bombastus von Hohenheim. The name *Bombastus* was appropriate, yet he assumed the name *Paracelsus*, which means "greater than Celsus," a physician in Rome during the first century C.E. From his early teens Paracelsus moved frequently between universities, gathering knowledge and moving on.

Portrait of Paracelsus in the Louvre Museum, Paris *(Ablestock/Jupiterimages)*

Over the years Paracelsus learned and practiced medicine, gaining respect despite his personality. Most of his ideas about healing and chemistry were wrong, but he managed to upset the rusted foundations of medicine and chemistry, which was still being taught based on Roman texts. The modern equivalent would be going to medical school and learning from a book published in 1000, forming *al-chemy*, or "the chemistry." Although analysis and transformation of gold and other materials was part of alchemy, from its inception there were strong religious, spiritual, and mystical branches and aspects to it. It was only in the 16th and 17th centuries that the practical superseded the mystical, corresponding with the eventual rise of chemistry as a science.

Alchemists were technologists who learned by experience and passed on what they learned to a select few. It was not of particular interest to them why techniques worked. As long as they did, that was good enough. As a result, innovation came slowly. From the forensic perspective the key contribution of the ancient alchemists was in their interest

before various plagues swept Europe. Science needed a good shaking up, and Paracelsus was the man to do it.

Paracelsus's work in medicinal chemistry led him to state, "What is there that is not poison? All things are poison and nothing [is] without poison. Solely the dose determines the thing that is not a poison." Without a fundamental chemical understanding of medicines, there was no way to know what the appropriate dose was. Above a threshold any therapeutic agent can become toxic and a poison. For its time this was a revolutionary idea and one that started a chain of events that led to effective tests for arsenic in the body. Paracelsus was one of the pioneers of experimental science when science was more philosophical than experimental.

Paracelsus cannot lay claim to being the father of forensic toxicology, but it is fair to call him one of its grandfathers. He created the groundwork for the broader field of toxicology both experimentally and philosophically. He wrote widely, and his works were popular and thus widely disseminated and studied. This is one of the first appearances of modern science. Existing understanding, even if faulty, formed the basis for the next round, leading (ideally) to a continually self-correcting and improving knowledge of the world.

in fire applied to metallurgy and the use of heat as a means of separating materials from one another. Centuries later, pyrochemistry was to play a role in the first viable tests for arsenic.

The ancient era of alchemy ended as the Roman Empire faded and Christianity rose. The church was hostile to science—what it perceived as paganism—and particularly to alchemy and its magical connotations. Several centuries passed before interest in science reawakened. Of most interest here are developments that coincided with the beginnings of the Renaissance. In the Western world a key figure during this period was a man named Paracelsus (1493–1541). He played an important role in the evolution of medicine to include more chemically derived medicines to supplement the plant-based ones that had predominated treatments from ancient times. His beliefs also were rooted in alchemy, particularly those practices related to the purification of metals. This interest set the stage for chemical separations, primitive analytical chemistry, the linkage of medicine to chemistry, and the emergence of chemistry as a recognized natural science. Some authors today credit Paracelsus with being the inspiration for forensic toxicology. During his lifetime it became clear that the tools of forensic toxicology were needed.

From Roman times well into the Victorian era poisoning was a recognized profession and a logical choice for committing and concealing murder. Up until the mid-1900s infectious disease was a common cause of death. The outward symptoms of a clever poisoning looked similar to those of a death caused by infections, typhus, dysentery, and other diseases rampant in those times. Investigators had to rely on observation of symptoms and circumstances rather than on scientific evidence. This state of affairs allowed many murderers to go unpunished and also sent many innocent people to prison or the gallows. Because it was rampant and because it was considered an easy crime to get away with, poisoning drove the development of forensic chemistry more than any other crime. Among poisons, one was the undisputed favorite. Work with this metal, starting in the 1400s, led to the birth of modern forensic toxicology.

ARSENIC

Arsenic poisoning commences the story of early forensic science. Arsenic (As) in its elemental form is a metal with an atomic number of 33 (33 protons in the nucleus) and an atomic weight of 74.9 atomic mass units.

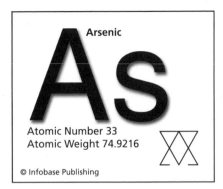

Atomic Number 33
Atomic Weight 74.9216

© Infobase Publishing

The symbols used for arsenic in alchemy and the modern periodic table of the elements. Arsenic is central to the history of forensic chemistry.

Because arsenic has two different oxidation states (arsenic III and arsenic V), it can exist in many solid and gaseous forms as well as dissolved in water. All of these different forms, sometimes referred to as species, have different toxicities, and they are usually divided into two groups: organic arsenic compounds (those containing carbon) and inorganic compounds (those without carbon). The organic forms of arsenic are generally less toxic than the inorganic forms. An example of organic form is methyl arsenic acid $CH_3AsO(OH)_2$.

The most famous form of arsenic as a poison is arsenic trioxide (As_2O_3), referred to as white arsenic or simply as arsenic. Dissolved in water, arsenic usually is found as an acid in the form of H_3AsO_3 (As III) and H_3AsO_4 (As V). Arsenic is found naturally in the body, but in very low amounts. People have always been exposed to arsenic in drinking water, but the degree of the exposure depends on the water's origin. Drinking water that comes from places where the soil has a high arsenic concentration, such as areas of Bangladesh, China, and the western United States, has higher concentrations of arsenic.

Arsenic has been an ingredient in medicines and cosmetics for at least 2,500 years. Preparations included treatments for skin disorders and syphilis, and as early as 400 B.C.E. it was used by the Greek physician Hippocrates to treat ulcers. Appearing in the late 1700s, a preparation known as Fowler's solution was used to treat skin problems, and later uses of arsenic focused on antimicrobial applications. This is no surprise; poisons are designed to kill, be it microbes, bugs, rats, or people. The use of arsenic as medicine was carried a bit too far in the late 1800s and early 1900s, when some people took arsenic in dilute preparations as a general health tonic. There were also legitimate uses of arsenic. Salvarsan, which contained arsenic, was the first effective treatment for syphilis, a sexually transmitted disease caused by bacteria.

It is not known when the poisonous nature of arsenic was discovered, but records of its use as a poison can be found as early as the fourth century B.C.E., during the Roman era. It was also during this period, in 82 B.C.E, that the first known law against poisoning was passed. From that period until the 1800s arsenic poisoning was widespread and difficult to detect or control. Some of the more famous poisoners include an Italian woman named Toffana, believed responsible for hundreds of deaths, and the Borgias, a prominent Italian family of the 15th and 16th centuries.

Arsenic was derived at that time from minerals and was widely available, but the identification and isolation of the element arsenic is credited to Albertus Magnus (ca. 1208–80), a German scholar, alchemist, and theologian. While there was still no clear understanding of the differences between compounds and elements, the isolation of metallic arsenic proved that the minerals that the Greeks thought were arsenic were in fact combinations of materials. In forensic terms Magnus was the first to use heat to drive off arsenic metal from the chemical matrix of a mineral. Five hundred years later the first forensic tests for arsenic would be based on this same principle.

Magnus noted that if sufficient heat is applied to minerals containing arsenic, the arsenic metal sublimes, which means that it evaporates directly to gas without going through a liquid phase. Magnus trapped this vapor and allowed the metal to condense. The same trick had been used for gold, but Magnus was the first to realize that there was such a thing as metallic arsenic and that a fire assay could be used to isolate it just as fire could be used to isolate and purify gold. For the time this was a significant insight. Gold exists as metallic gold in nature: It usually does not look like gold locked up in ores or rocks.

Magnus, also known as Albert the Great, is notable for other contributions. He became a professor at the University of Paris and counted among his students Thomas Aquinas. He also rose to the rank of bishop in a time when early science and religion were uneasy bedfellows at best. He is quoted with saying, "The aim of natural science is not simply to accept the statements of others, but to investigate the causes that are at work in nature," a sentiment remarkable for its time. As an alchemist, Aquinas was adept at using nitric acid as a means of separating gold from silver. A similar technique would be central in separating arsenic from forensic samples a few centuries later.

Once arsenic could be chemically separated from other materials, the stage was set for dramatic breakthroughs that would gradually spell the end of murder by arsenic poisoning. In 1752 science was applied to an arsenic poisoning case in England, in which a young woman named Mary Blandy was suspected of poisoning her father.

The Case of Mary Blandy

Mary Blandy (ca. 1719–52) was a woman with a problem: Her father disapproved of the man she wanted to marry. To remove the obstacle she allegedly poisoned her father in 1751 with the help of her fiancé, who provided the arsenic powder. Apparently, Mary's first attempt to add the poison to her father's tea failed. The powder formed a film on the surface of the hot liquid, and he refused to drink it. Next, her father and two household employees fell ill after consuming gruel prepared in the house. Because three people showed symptoms of arsenic poisoning, the incident was suspicious and led to an investigation.

The pot used to cook the gruel was the key piece of physical evidence. A government investigator used several tests to determine simple physical and chemical characteristics of a white residue left in the pan to determine that it was arsenic. One test involved heating the powder and noting a strong odor like garlic, characteristic of arsenic, but not conclusive proof of its presence. This and other simple tests led the investigator to conclude that the powder was arsenic. Mary Blandy was arrested, tried, and convicted for the murder of her father. She was executed by hanging in April 1752. Among her last words was a request to the hangman not to hang her too high, for modesty's sake. Although the scientific tests used in this case were primitive by modern standards, they were among the first recorded use of scientific tests to detect and identify a poisonous material.

JAMES MARSH AND THE MARSH TEST

An important test used in early toxicology was developed in 1836 by chemist James Marsh (1794–1846), nearly 80 years after the Mary Blandy case. The Blandy case marked the beginning of a wider reliance on and demand for trustworthy scientific tests for detection of poisons. Shortly after Blandy's execution Swedish chemist Carl Wilhelm Scheele (1742–86) developed a postmortem test for arsenic. Scheele was an apothecary's assistant and an excellent technician who discovered the element chlorine. His arsenic test involved heating arsenic powder (As_2O_3) placed in a solution containing metallic zinc and nitric acid. The arsenic formed the arsine gas AsH_3 that smelled of garlic, a test that was used in many cases, including that of Blandy. Other chemists improved and enhanced this test and attempted to extend it to use on human tissues and stomach contents. These early methods were difficult, required great skill, and could not detect relatively low levels of arsenic. A famous case revealed this limitation to light and brought English chemist Marsh into the story.

In 1832 John Bodle had been accused of poisoning his grandfather with arsenic placed in coffee. Marsh was asked by the prosecution to check the stomach contents of the victim. He used a hydrogen sulfide method and was able to produce a yellow solid consistent with the presence of arsenic. Unfortunately, the solid degraded between the time it was prepared and when it was presented to a jury. To Marsh's dismay Bodle was acquitted. To add insult to injury Bodle later bragged about his guilt. Marsh took his anger and frustration and disappeared into his lab with one simple goal: develop a reliable and visually convincing method to detect arsenic in messy and complex samples like tissue and stomach contents.

First, he turned to Scheele's procedure in which arsenic was converted to arsine gas. Marsh knew that under the proper conditions compounds containing arsenic, such as arsine, could be manipulated to form arsenic metal. Magnus had demonstrated that conversion centuries earlier. Marsh realized that metallic arsenic is stable, and if he could capture the arsine gas, he could manipulate it so that metallic arsenic would form on a solid surface. This process is sometimes called "plating out." This simple idea took Marsh four years to perfect, and the method became known as the Marsh test. This famous procedure was the first reliable

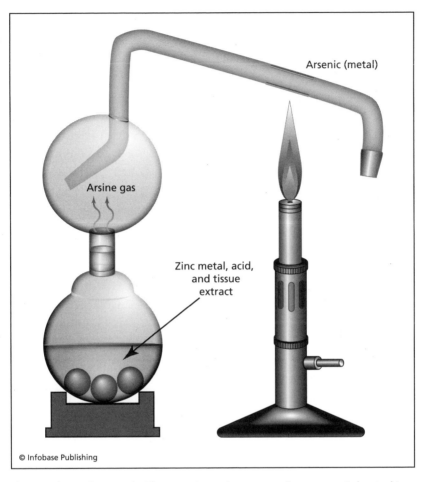

The Marsh test for arsenic. The sample, such as stomach contents, is heated in the presence of zinc metal and acid. The arsine gas rises into the glass tube. With more heating arsenic metal forms a metallic mirror on the tube.

analytical test for arsenic. For his efforts Marsh received wide acclaim and a gold medal from the Royal Society of Arts.

The Marsh test starts by placing the sample, be it a powder, stomach contents, or body tissue, in solution by adding hydrochloric acid. Shavings of metallic zinc are included in the mixture, which is then heated. Under these conditions arsenic forms arsine gas (H_3As) that rises away from solution. The innovation Marsh added was to trap this gas and direct it through a tube. The gas is heated again, causing the arsine gas to decompose to metallic arsenic, which plates out a gray coating on glass or on a piece of porcelain. Unlike the arsenic compound formed with hydrogen sulfide gas, the metallic "mirror" is stable and makes ideal visual evidence for display before a jury. One critical feature of the Marsh test was that it was fairly reliable when used on biological samples.

The Marsh test came to the public's attention during the case of Marie Lafarge (1840) and was particularly notable because of who used it, a man named M. J. B. Orfila (1787–1853). Owing to his skills in forensic toxicology and his role in this case, Orfila is often referred to as the father of forensic toxicology.

The Lafarge case revolved around the death of Marie's husband, Charles, who died of an illness that was consistent with arsenic poisoning. Initial tests of his stomach showed no arsenic, nor did other organs removed from the body. However, arsenic was detected in food and beverages that Charles had been given. The court asked Orfila, a recognized expert in forensic toxicology, to sort out the analytical results. He and other experts reviewed and reanalyzed the samples, finding small amounts of arsenic in the remains of Charles Lafarge. Orfila, a consummate chemist, also showed that the arsenic could not be attributed to the soil in which the body had been buried or to contaminated reagents. To this day such awareness of possible contamination and the use of control samples are an integral part of forensic toxicology. The Lafarge case was pivotal for forensic chemistry, forensic toxicology, and forensic science. It marked the first time that modern chemical testing was used, accepted, and instrumental in obtaining a conviction in a murder case. From that moment poisoning was no longer easy to mistake for other causes of death.

Orfila's testimony and the acceptance of the Marsh test by the scientific and legal communities did not end poisoning, nor did it help prevent accidental exposures to arsenic. As is often the case, the scientific advance it highlighted provided great assistance to law enforcement but also forced those who would break the law to alter their tactics. The Marsh test made arsenic poisoning a less attractive means of murder, so murderers moved on to other poisons, such as those obtained from plants.

The most common plant-based poisons are chemically classified as alkaloids. These substances were originally called "vegetable bases" as they were extracted from plants and the extracts were found to be basic, or alkaline. A basic substance tastes bitter and when dissolved in water will cause the pH of a solution to rise above 7.0. A pH of 7 is neutral, 0-6 acidic, and above 7, basic. Examples of alkaloids include nicotine,

M. J. B. Orfila: The Father of Forensic Toxicology

Mathieu Joseph Bonaventure (Mateu Josep Bonaventura) Orfila (1787–1853) was born in Catalonia, Spain, but as a medical student moved to France, where he worked and became professor of forensic chemistry and dean of the medical faculty at the University of Paris. He began publishing articles describing his work early in his career; his first paper on poisons appeared in 1814, when he was 26 years old.

Orfila spent a good deal of time studying poisons, particularly arsenic. As a toxicologist, he concentrated on methods of analyzing poisons in blood and other body fluids and tissues. He became involved in the Lafarge case in 1840.

Lithograph of M. J. B. Orfila
(National Library of Medicine)

Initial results of the analysis of Charles Lafarge's remains were negative for arsenic, but Orfila was eventually able to detect arsenic in the exhumed remains. He was dogged in his work, detail oriented, and, in many ways, ahead of his time. For example, he realized that because Charles had been buried for some time, arsenic found naturally in the soil might contaminate the remains and cause misleading results. Orfila took care to test the soil and showed that the levels found in the dead man exceeded the amount that could have come from the soil. The dead man's widow, Marie Lafarge, was eventually convicted of poisoning her husband after a long and highly publicized trial. Orfila's testimony in the case was one of the earliest examples of sound scientific testimony by a recognized scientific expert in a court of law.

morphine, cocaine, atropine, and thebaine. In large doses these compounds act as poisons that in the mid-1800s were almost impossible to identify. Alkaloids are difficult to extract from tissue, making the task of detection even more of a challenge for early toxicologists.

A breakthrough in combating alkaloid poisoning came in 1850 as part of an investigation of a suspicious death in which the suspected killers had doused the body with vinegar. The man responsible for this advance was Belgian Jean Servais Stas (1813–91). Stas quickly realized that the presence of vinegar on the body was an important clue. When an acid is mixed with a base, the result is neutralization of both. Perhaps, Stas reasoned, the killers tried to neutralize an alkaloid poison using the vinegar. After lengthy experiments on the body tissues preserved from the victim, Stas developed a procedure to extract alkaloid poisons. Eventually, he was able to identify nicotine as the poison used in the case. He reported the results to authorities, who investigated further. Investigators quickly determined that the suspects had extracted large amounts of tobacco in the days leading to the murder. Bodies of animals used in experiments by the murderers were also found. Two people, a man and a woman, were arrested and convicted of murder.

Marsh, Orfila, and Stas were pioneers of forensic science, particularly forensic chemistry. Their advances did not stop poisoning, but the number of cases dropped as scientific tests improved. In the 20th century forensic chemists improved their ability to isolate and identify poisons as well as accurately determine the quantities of poisons and their metabolic by-products in blood, urine, and other body fluids and tissues. Toxicologists are still confronted with suicidal and accidental chronic poisoning from exposure to arsenic at low levels in drinking water, food, or soil. One or two doses are not harmful, but over time these doses accumulate and can cause disease and death. Poisoning as a method of murder, however, is now exceedingly rare.

2

Scientific Principles, Instrumentation, and Equipment

The tools of the modern analytical chemist began to emerge in the 1600s as simple, even primitive, tests that relied on little more than a color change as a positive result. Later developments were tests that integrated the separation of compounds with detection, similar to the Marsh test, which separated arsenic from tissues. Simple separations and detection were the mainstays of forensic chemists from Orfila's time to the middle of the 20th century. It is only within the last 60 years that instrumentation has become the core of forensic testing and only within the last 20 years that computer-enabled automation has become common. Still, many modern forensic tests begin with simple color tests and end with sophisticated instruments. In a sense this approach is a replay of the history of the tools and techniques used by forensic chemists.

EARLY ANALYTICAL TECHNIQUES: WET CHEMISTRY

Chemistry was born from the study of drugs and medicine, but analytical chemistry sprang from the study of metals. Once ancient

All possible components

Presumptive tests

Screening tests

Definitive identification

Quantitative analysis

The "flow" of a forensic analysis. The goal is to narrow down the possibilities to the smallest size possible or to one single compound.

© Infobase Publishing

peoples recognized the value of precious metals such as gold and silver, they required methods for detecting and validating purity. Chemists learned to use heat to extract gold and silver from raw ores and materials, a technique that is still part of modern metallurgy. Those skilled in these arts were the first analytical chemists, and their techniques are now referred to as dry chemical techniques since no solutions were used to separate the metals. In fact, all that was required was a very hot fire.

The first wet methods for the analysis of metals and gold were published in the early 1500s. The wet method was so named because the sample of metal was dissolved in a water-based solution such as a strong acid. By making and weighing a compound with a known percentage of the metal, it was relatively easy to calculate the amount of the metal in the original sample. The only instrument needed was a reliable balance to weigh the initial sample and final product. Since the resulting product falls out of solution to form a solid, this type of wet chemical method is called a gravimetric method. Gravimetric analyses are still used today and most students who take chemistry in college still perform gravimetric laboratory experiments to learn laboratory fundamentals. From the forensic perspective these methods are important because they represent the first separation techniques.

Gravimetric methods were among the first that were both quantitative and qualitative, meaning that it was possible to determine both what was present in a sample (qualitative) and how much (quantitative). Both capabilities are still crucial in forensic chemistry. The early dry heating methods used to separate metals were crude, and quantitative results were not reliable. However, once chemists learned

Gold

Gold (Au) is a precious metal, meaning that even in ancient times people recognized that it has special properties and is extremely rare. The symbol Au comes from the Latin word *aurum*. Aside from its beautiful appearance, gold does not tarnish. Chemically this means that gold does not react with oxygen (O_2) in the air, so it retains its lustrous appearance over time. Gold also does not react with water or many acids or bases, so it is extremely durable. For this reason gold is frequently used as a catalyst or for wiring in specialized instruments and devices in addition to its use in jewelry and currency. It is not known when people began to use gold as a sign of wealth, but it was mentioned in ancient Egyptian texts dating back nearly 3,000 years. Gold is soft and extremely malleable, which means that it can be hammered into very thin sheets. For making jewelry or coins, especially using ancient tools and techniques, this is an important property. Dentists also utilize gold for making fillings and other dental appliances.

The role of gold in the story of forensic chemistry relates to how people tested for it. Once gold was used to represent wealth, people needed to know how pure a particular nugget or coin was to assign a proper value. At first this was nearly impossible because chemists did not know how to separate gold from other materials. The first methods that worked involved fire, in which the metal was heated to drive off impurities. It was not until the Middle Ages that acids became available and chemists learned how to dissolve solid samples. Once they were dissolved, chemists could devise tests to detect the presence and quantity of gold in the sample. The need to separate gold from other materials was an important factor in the development of analytical chemistry.

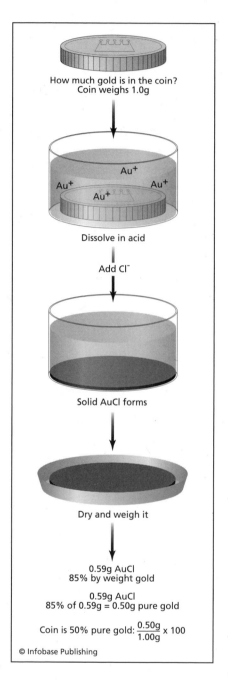

How much gold is in the coin?
Coin weighs 1.0g

Dissolve in acid

Add Cl⁻

Solid AuCl forms

Dry and weigh it

0.59g AuCl
85% by weight gold

0.59g AuCl
85% of 0.59g = 0.50g pure gold

Coin is 50% pure gold: $\frac{0.50g}{1.00g}$ x 100

© Infobase Publishing

A coin weighing a gram contains gold, but how much? Chemists in the 1500s could use an acid to dissolve the coin. They could then add a reagent that would form an insoluble solid with the gold, such as gold chloride (AuCl), which chemists knew is 85 percent gold by weight. They next dried the solid and weighed it. Since this solid is 85 percent gold, the coin contained 85 percent of the total weight of the solid, 0.59 gram in this case, of gold, or about half a gram. The coin is 50 percent pure.

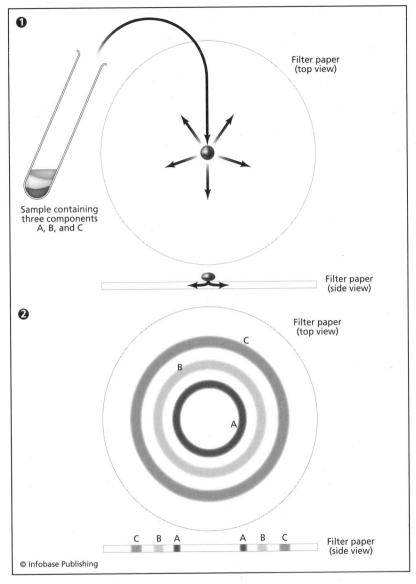

❶

Filter paper
(top view)

Sample containing
three components
A, B, and C

Filter paper
(side view)

❷

Filter paper
(top view)

C

B

A

C B A   A B C   Filter paper
(side view)

© Infobase Publishing

Spot tests. A drop of the dissolved sample is applied to a piece of filter
paper and immediately diffuses outward. In this example there are three
components in the mixture, and each moves at a different speed. When
the analysis is complete, the three components are separated by distance
traveled.

to perform separations based on dissolution using wet chemistry, advances quickly followed in both qualitative and quantitative analytical chemistry.

An important test for modern forensic chemistry, spot testing, appeared in the 1800s. To perform a spot test the chemist dissolves a sample that might contain several compounds in a water solution. A tiny drop is applied to the center of a piece of paper so that the solution is concentrated at this one small point. The sample diffuses outward with the individual components in the sample moving at different speeds. As a result the components also travel different distances. The distance depends on the compound and how much it interacted with the paper matrix; the more it interacts, the slower it moves. A spot test can be modified by impregnating the filter paper with chemical reagents that would react selectively with different components in the sample. This approach of separation followed by detection is still used in modern separations. Spot testing reached a peak in the early 1900s when several books were published on the subject.

As instrument methods (discussed later in the chapter) were developed, the role of simple spot tests changed. In modern forensic chemistry labs the analysts initially use simple qualitative tests to narrow down the list of substances that might be present in evidence. Many of these qualitative tests are based on the formation of colored compounds and are often referred to as color tests. Many chemists still call simple qualitative tests "spot tests" even though the methods differ from earlier versions. Genuine spot tests survive in the modern lab in the form of chromatography, particularly a technique called thin-layer chromatography, which is discussed in a later section.

CHEMISTRY OF COLOR

One way chemists know that a chemical reaction has occurred is by seeing a change in color. Forensic chemists use color change tests (color tests) to determine what an unknown sample may contain. A color test is usually performed by placing a small amount of the sample into a well on a plate or into a test tube. Special chemical solutions are added, and any change in color is noted. A change in color indicates that a change has occurred in the molecules that make up the sample.

The organic molecule carotene, which imparts an orange color to carrots. The color arises from the way light interacts with the alternating double bonds between carbon atoms.

Broadly speaking, there are two types of chemicals that produce color. Organic compounds that contain carbon and hydrogen molecules can be colored if they also have a pattern of alternating double bonds between carbons. Most dyes are based on this type of structure. When a color test reagent is added to a sample containing drug molecules, chemical changes can result in the formation of compounds that contain alternating double bonds. If this happens, a color develops or an existing color changes.

The other way a color can be produced is by a unique chemical structure called a complex. Complexes form between ions of metals such as cobalt (Co) and compounds that have nitrogen and oxygen atoms. Many drugs have nitrogens in their structure and can form colored complexes with metal ions. The color test used for cocaine and related drugs is based on cobalt, which forms a deep blue complex with cocaine. Color change reactions like this are used in many aspects of forensic chemistry.

If blood and death belonged to the English and the Americans, forensic chemistry belonged to the Germans and the Austrians. Much of this heritage is unappreciated outside Europe, given language barriers and the lack of English translations of many pioneering papers. Once the Stas-Otto method had provided the means to extract poisons from tissues, the issue of which poison was present remained. This led to color-based tests that were used to tease out likely identities. The color produced in most tests is the result of dye formation. Many of the earliest tests developed to screen for certain drugs and toxins carry the name of the people who developed them, including Marquis (a student of the German chemist Kobert), Dragendorff, Mecke, Ehrlich, Frohde, Liebermann, and Zwikker. Most of these tests were described in publications from 1870 to 1905. Forensic chemists and law-enforcement officers still use these tests today. In the 1960s and the 1970s German chemists published articles describing how the color tests worked on a molecular level.

This litany of names shows how German chemists excelled in two areas intimately related to forensic science—dyes and drugs. There is a neat symmetry here; the color tests mentioned earlier work, in many cases, by forming a dye; many drugs were made accidentally while the chemists were busy trying to make dyes, and vice versa. Explosives manufacturing closely connected to both. It might seem that drugs and dyes have little in common with each other, but chemically, these families share common roots. Drugs are of obvious forensic importance, but the role of dyes is less so.

Dyes, along with pigments, are colorants that impart color to the substrate to which they are applied. Solubility dictates the distinction between them; dyes dissolve in solution like food coloring in water, while pigments form a suspension in solution and dry as a coating on a surface. The chemical structure alone does not automatically dictate which is which, because a change in solvent can change solubility. The forensic importance of dyes and pigments, particularly from a chemical point of view, is a recent development that traces back to the introduction of materials that use them. Pigments are widely used in paints and inks and as colorants for fabrics and fibers. It is this last application that spurred the chemical developments that would have the greatest impact on forensic science.

The mention of dyes appeared during 3000–2000 B.C.E. The dye compounds came from extracts of plants, leaves, and other colored materials. The ancients derived pigments for paints by grinding up colored minerals and suspending them in water or other slurry materials. The Chinese and the Egyptians made inks and paints using charcoal suspended in oils or animal fats. Along with medicines and metallurgy, interest in colorants was a primary driver of early chemistry. Once beyond simple extracts and slurries, progress in colorant chemistry had to wait for techniques of chemical synthesis to evolve, a process that picked up dramatic speed in the late 1800s.

Many naturally derived drugs share chemical similarities with naturally derived dyes. The alkaloids, for example, a class of drugs that include heroin, morphine, and cocaine as well as thousands of others, are based on a structure called a tertiary amine. Indigo, the dye used to make blue jeans blue, also contains tertiary amine groups. The first synthetic dye created, mauve, was an accidental by-product of an attempt to make quinine to treat malaria. It is not surprising, then, that the chemical histories of drugs and dyes run parallel. Before the advent of synthetic organic chemistry, drugs and dyes could only be obtained from natural sources, such as extracts, teas, and mineral preparations. Chemists lacked that knowledge and tools to create new molecules and, thus, new drugs from precursors.

Drug chemistry diverges from that of dyes in an important and obvious way: People can abuse drugs. Pinning down the definition of abused drugs begs a definition of abuse. This is a social rather than a scientific question, the answer to which depends on the circumstance and the place in history. The Sumerians and Egyptians were excellent brewers, with the former showing a penchant for brewing beer, while the Egyptians were particularly adept at wine making. Hair analysis from ancient samples from Peru revealed the presence of metabolites of cocaine, which supports the notion that chewing coca leaves began in South America around 2000 B.C.E., if not earlier. Marijuana was mentioned in Chinese texts from the third century B.C.E., and because the marijuana (hemp) plant is hardy (i.e., a weed), it grows almost anywhere. It is not surprising that use of its products was widespread in the ancient world. The pursuit of medicines and treatments remained separate from chemistry until Paracelsus and his followers began to bring chemistry into the search for medicines, a search that predictably led to the discovery of drugs of abuse. What was not predictable was that dye chemists would be the ones leading the way.

Of all the colors, the most sought after in ancient times were the blues and the purples. Indigo, one of the earliest blue dyes comes from the *Indigofera tinctoria* plant. The leaves and their extracts are not blue and require chemical processing for the blue color to emerge. The extract is first soaked in a basic solution and then oxidized by exposure to air. Likely, this was an accidental discovery, but the realization that colors could be coaxed from colorless materials was a chemically important step, even if ancient dye makers did not understand the fundamental chemistry they were practicing.

Chemists exploited indigo for analytical purposes in the 1800s. A reagent consisting of indigo dissolved in sulfuric acid. If the sample contained nitric acid, the indigo was bleached from the characteristic blue to a clear solution. The test was used forensically in the early 1800s until William Brooke O'Shaughnessy (1809–89), published his first paper in the medical journal *The Lancet* in 1830, describing the shortcomings of the test. This was important because some poisoners used nitric acid. O'Shaughnessy, who was 21 when he wrote the report, pointed out that other compounds besides nitric acid reacted with indigo. In noting this, he was contradicting some of the early English forensic scientists of note, including Robert Christison, who had a medical degree from the University of Edinburgh. It was a courageous action for such a young chemist.

Not satisfied with debunking the existing method, O'Shaughnessy described three tests that were specific for nitric acid: first, nitric acid would turn orange in the presence of morphine (forming another dye); second, it would form a solid when added to urea nitrate; and third, it would facilitate formation of silver fulminate. Detection of the latter was simple, obvious, and hazardous. In publishing the paper, O'Shaughnessy was following Christison's advice to forensic chemists that it was the job of the analyst to provide more than some evidence but to provide the best evidence possible given the limits of scientific knowledge of the time. For a short period, indigo dye and other tests represented those limits.

Another famous ancient dye was royal purple, also called Tyrian purple for the coastal city where its manufacture was centralized. Tyre, once part of the ancient Phoenician Empire, is on the coast of Lebanon, a city build on mounds of mollusk shells used in the production of the dye. The process of making Tyrian purple started by gathering mollusks and extracting their glands. Next, the extracted material oxidized to form

William Brooke O'Shaughnessy: A Pioneer in Pharmacology

Sir William Brooke O'Shaughnessy (1809–89) was a British forensic chemist who enjoyed a wide-ranging career. He took on a project in 1830 at the request of the editor of the prestigious medical journal *The Lancet* related to a rash of poisonings seemingly traceable to candy. Ever the methodical chemist, he developed a systematic method of testing for the presence of organic and inorganic poisons that found their way into candy by accident or design. Mindful of the tendency of children to suck on the candy wrappers, he considered those as a possible mode of ingestion. He eventually identified a number of contaminants and adulterants, including compounds containing lead, antimony, mercury, copper, and the dye Prussian blue. His findings led to further investigation of adulterated products, with offenders having their names published in *The Lancet*.

O'Shaughnessy joined the East India Company as an assistant surgeon and went to Calcutta, India, in 1833. He had wanted to return to his practice of medicine, but his forensic chemical skills kept interfering with this plan. In India, he was given the post of chemical examiner at Calcutta Medical College. This assignment was in addition to his medical duties. It was there that he demonstrated the Marsh test and began to use it. He also was among the first to point out one of its shortcomings, such as the potential for antimony to react similarly to arsenic, leading to a false positive result.

O'Shaughnessy's contributions to forensic chemistry were among many other accomplishments. As a doctor, he championed the use of cannabis (marijuana) to English medical practice as a treatment for tetanus, cholera, and convulsive problems. Having worked with many cholera victims early in his career, he became adept at looking at stomach contents and judging if a death was due to a disease or arsenic poisoning. In India he became an assayer at the Calcutta Mint and was instrumental in bringing telegraphic service to the country. He wrote a book on forensic chemistry in the form of a medical manual for students in Calcutta and was knighted in 1856.

the final color, much like with indigo. The process required thousands of purple snails to make any appreciable amount of dye, and it is not surprising the species nearly became extinct. The dye was one of the most valuable commodities in the ancient world. Alizarin was another ancient dye, red in color.

The dye industry was central to manufacturing and trade from the ancient times until well into the 19th century. The nature of the manufacturing process was labor- and material-intensive, making dyes too expensive for most people to afford. In the 1700s interest turned to finding ways to synthesize dyes from cheaper and more abundant resources. One of the first to try was Peter Woulfe, who began with indigo in 1771. He treated it with nitric acid to make picric acid, a lovely yellow compound. Its dye applications were short-lived. When dry, picric acid is unstable and detonates easily, a generally undesirable feature for clothing. Regardless, the recognition that dyes could be converted to other dyes with chemical treatments was an important step forward, even if picric acid (thankfully) never made a significant impact on the dye industry.

In 1858 Johann Peter Griess (1829–88), a German chemist, described a type of reaction called diazotization in which an amine compound (one containing an -NH_2 group) reacts with nitrite ion (NO_2^-) under acidic conditions to yield diazonium salts that are often highly colored. The reaction can continue further to coupling reactions that produce highly colored products. Uncovering the reaction led to production of azo dyes by 1861. The coupling reactions, often considered a nuisance in salt production, have been utilized extensively in forensic chemistry as color-based presumptive tests for drugs and in other forensic applications.

For much of the last century, the Griess test was one of the principal screening tests used for detection of gunshot residue (GSR). In this test, the analyte of interest is not the amine but the nitrite, which is a by-product of combustion of gunpowder. An acidic solution of the starting amine (naphthylamine) is added to the sample suspected of containing gunshot residue. If nitrite is present, the dye formation proceeds to yield a red dye. A modified version detects nitrates (NO_3^-) in water. The source of this material is usually runoff water containing fertilizers, which are high in nitrates. Ammonium nitrate (NH_4NO_3) is one of the main culprits and is used as an ingredient in explosives. The bomb used in Oklahoma City explosion in 1995 was made of ANFO, a combination of ammonium nitrate and fuel oil.

Griess did not actually make the first synthetic dye. That honor goes to William Henry Perkin (1838–1907), mentioned briefly above. He was an 18-year-old chemist who was working to improve treatments for malaria. He was interested in making quinine, which at the time (1856) was the only known effective treatment for the disease. Quinine was made from extracts of coal tar in a complex process that Perkins hoped to sidestep by starting from simpler ingredients. He did not succeed in that quest, but he did manage to create an intense purple-blue solution that not only dyed cloth but also did not weather, fade, or wash out. He quickly abandoned the quest for quinine, patented the dye, called mauveine (mauve), and started a company in London called Perkin & Son. The name was a gesture of gratitude to his father, who helped fund his work. Perkin's contribution to dye chemistry was to show that it was possible to start from compounds found in coal tar. This and other related materials were and remain relatively cheap and abundant. This freed the dye chemists from scarce and costly natural materials such as plants, mollusks, and other living precursors.

By 1868 Carl Liebermann and others had created colorants consisting of metals and dyes. They understood that the key structural feature of dyes responsible for color was a series of alternating double bonds, such as those found in mauve. Knowing this, Liebermann was able to focus his efforts. During the 1870s and 1880s, he developed color tests based on dye formation and remained a central figure in early colorant and dye chemistry. The Liebermann test is still used occasionally to detect the presence of phenol groups (benzene rings with -OH attached, as in aspirin). A positive reaction produces a colored dye product. The Ehrlich reagent (1901) consists of p-dimethylaminobenzaldehyde, which reacts with indoles such as LSD and mescaline to form colored dyes, purple in the case of LSD.

Paul Ehrlich (1854–1915) was one of the more productive and colorful of the color chemists. He often carried a box of cigars under one arm, of which he smoked about 25 a day. He was also reported to eat little and to frequent beer halls, where he got into spirited discussions and debates. Despite—or because of—this eccentricity, he won a Nobel Prize in medicine in 1908 for work related to both medicine and dyes. He worked with stains used to color tissues and microorganisms. His work in the late 1880s was the foundation of the Gram staining procedure still used today to differentiate bacterial types. In the 1890s Ehrlich turned his attention to immunological work and later to medicine and pharmacology. He screened hundreds of compounds to treat the spirochete that was known to cause syphilis. Prior to his work, mercury was the only viable treatment for the disease, resulting in many fatalities. After screening more than 600 compounds, Ehrlich identified one that contained arsenic and became known as salvarsan, discussed previously. Another German dye-making company, Hoechst Dye Works, marketed the drug starting in 1910. In a replay of the Baeyer aspirin story, the success of the drug allowed the company to move more aggressively into pharmaceuticals.

Perhaps the most versatile color test used in forensic drug analysis is the Marquis test published in 1896. The ingredients are simple—formaldehyde and sulfuric acid. The Marquis reagent reacts with many alkaloid drugs to form a variety of colors. Amphetamine and methamphetamine create orange dyes, while the opiates react with the reagent to form purple ones. Ninhydrin, a common reagent used for visualizing fingerprints, was introduced in the early 1900s and reacts with the amino acids to form a purple-colored dye. As a result of the rapid advances in the late 1800s, forensic chemists entered the 1900s with a rich assortment of extraction and detection methods, all based on classical wet chemistry.

Chemists now know that the results of color tests are not absolute and there is always more than one compound that can produce what appears to be a positive result. If a chemist tests a substance with a color test reagent and sees a characteristic color change, the best way to interpret the result is "more likely than not." The sample more likely than not contains the substance of interest, but it is not certain. The analyst must always be mindful of false positives, in which a substance that is not the target produces the color change. Similarly, if a test reagent should cause a color change and does not, this is called a false negative. All presumptive tests are conducted with these possibilities in mind, and it is why all preliminary findings are confirmed with other techniques.

FLOW OF FORENSIC ANALYSIS

When a chemist receives a powdered or other solid sample for analysis, the first thing he or she usually does is take a few milligrams of the material and test it with several reagents. The color change observed, if there is one, provides the analyst with a reasonable idea of the sample's contents. The analyst will also have a good idea of what is not present, but the results are not conclusive. If the reagent used to test for cocaine (cobalt thiocyanate) gives a positive color change (turning from pink to blue), this means that the sample more likely than not contains cocaine or a compound related to it. Further tests will prove or disprove this hypothesis. In the field police officers used color tests to determine if a suspicious powder might contain an illegal or dangerous substance. The modern forensic chemist has an arsenal of color tests to choose from, as shown in the table on page 28.

THIN-LAYER CHROMATOGRAPHY

The original spot tests were the basis of another technique that is used in forensic chemistry, thin-layer chromatography (TLC). This technique was developed in the 1800s and led to many advances in sample preparation and, eventually, in instrumentation. *Chromatography* means "color writing," and the word is thought to relate to early experiments in which plant pigments were separated this way. All chromatography, including TLC, is based on the idea of selective partitioning between two phases. Although it sounds exotic, partitioning is something everyone is familiar with, even if they do not realize it. Vinaigrette salad dressing is a mixture of oil and vinegar, two liquid phases that are not soluble in each other. Vinegar is a solution of dilute acetic acid in water. Even when shaken, the oil and water will eventually separate into two distinct layers.

Now consider table salt, which is sodium chloride (NaCl). Salt dissolves easily in water but not in oil. If salt is added to the salad dressing and the dressing is shaken, the salt will end up in the watery vinegar solution and not in the oil layer, since salt dissolves in water but not significantly in oil. This is an example of partitioning. The salt has greater affinity for the water and will end up in the water phase. There may be traces of salt left in the oil, but the concentration of salt in oil would be very small. The same would happen if sugar were added to the oil-vinegar mix; sugar is soluble in water and not in oil, so the sugar would end up in the water phase.

Which compounds will dissolve in a given solvent depends on the chemical structure of compounds involved. For example, table salt

PRESUMPTIVE TESTS (COLOR TESTS) USED IN FORENSIC CHEMISTRY

Drug, evidence, or analyte	Color test	Color change (positive)
amphetamine/ methamphetamine	Mandelin's/Marquis	green/orange-brown
barbiturates	Dilli-Kopanyi	red
	Zwikker's	purple
benzodiazepines	Zimmerman	purplish-pink
cocaine	cobalt thiocyanate	silvery blue
	Liebermann's	yellow
heroin	Froehdes	purple
	Liebermann's	black
	Marquis	purple
LSD	Erlich's	purple
	UV light	fluorescence
marijuana and related	Duquenois-Levine	purple
	Froehdes	green or yellow
mescaline	Mandelin's	green
	Marquis	orange
morphine	Marquis	purple
	Liebermann's	black
mescaline (peyote)	Marquis	orange
	Froehdes	green
psilocin/psilocybin	Ehrlich's	gray or purple
	Marquis	orange or yellow

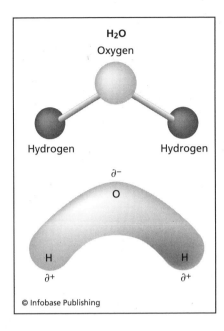

H_2O

Oxygen

Hydrogen   Hydrogen

∂^-

O

H   H

∂^+ ∂^+

© Infobase Publishing

Water molecules have what is called a permanent dipole because the electron cloud surrounding it is unevenly distributed. Water is classified as a polar molecule because of it. It is often drawn as a boomerang shape to show how the charges are oriented on the molecule. Dipoles are something like Earth's North and South Poles or the positive and negative terminals on a battery. Because of this permanent separation of charges, water dissolves many ionic compounds, as well as other polar compounds. This is an example of the principle of "like dissolves like."

is an ionic compound, meaning that it consists of positively charged sodium ions (Na^+) and negatively charged chloride ions (Cl^-). Water is a polar molecule that has partial charges. Because of this, water can dissolve many ionic compounds. Oil contains long chains of hydrocarbon molecules that repel water; therefore, oil and water are not miscible (they will not mix or dissolve in each other). The basis of this type of partitioning is a principle informally referred to as "like dissolves like."

The way partitioning works in TLC is more complex than the salt-oil-water example. The first phase is the solvent mixture (a mobile liquid), and the second is the paper, which is stationary. When the solvent reaches the sample spot on a piece of paper, anything that can dissolve will dissolve and move with the solvent. As the solvent front moves forward, the dissolved compounds can do one of two things: stay in the paper matrix or move with the solvent. The more affinity they have for the solvent, the faster they will move up the paper. The more affinity they have for the paper, the slower they will move, and the closer they will remain to the original spot or origin. Similar principles were exploited in the spot tests described earlier. The end result is separation of the

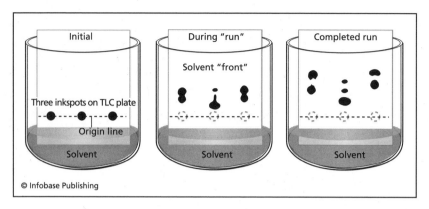

| Initial | During "run" | Completed run |

Solvent "front"

Three inkspots on TLC plate

Origin line

Solvent | Solvent | Solvent

© Infobase Publishing

Thin-layer chromatography (TLC). The sample drop is placed near the bottom of the paper (the origin) and allowed to dry. The paper is placed upright in a shallow solvent mixture. Like water absorbed into a paper towel, the solvent is drawn up the paper and encounters the spot. The components in the spot that dissolve in the solvent move up the paper with it and separate.

components of the mixture if the solvent and paper have the proper chemical structures to effect that separation.

Modern TLC is performed on plates of glass or plastic coated with a powdery solid. These solid phases are designed to have affinities for different materials. By selecting different TLC plates, a chemist can separate a larger variety of compounds than could be done with paper alone. An instrument called a densitometer can be used to measure the density of the spots on the plate when the analysis is complete. The denser a spot, the more material is present. Such an observation provides what is called semi-quantitative information. Hundreds of solvent combinations have been tried over the years, and specialized developing sprays are used to develop spots that might otherwise be invisible.

As useful as TLC is, by the middle of the 20th century chemists needed more powerful techniques to separate and identify compounds. This need, along with advances in technology around the time of World War II, spurred the invention of instrumental methods of analysis that have become the heart of forensic chemistry. Nonetheless, the one instrument that many forensic scientists consider to be their most valuable tool was invented nearly 400 years ago.

DEVELOPMENT OF INSTRUMENTAL TECHNIQUES

Many people think of large, expensive, and exotic room-filling machines when they think of chemical instruments, yet this is an uncommon sight in modern forensic labs. The first police laboratory, which was established by Edmund Locard (1877–1966) in 1910 in Lyon, France, reportedly had two types of instruments: microscopes and spectrophotometers.

Microscopes are not usually considered instruments in the modern sense, but they were one of the first pieces of equipment available to chemists and forensic chemists. Without microscopes there would be no forensic science. Interestingly, a trip to a modern forensic chemistry lab reveals an abundance of two types of devices—microscopes and spectrophotometers—and combinations of the two. These two devices are related in other ways as well. Both use energy (light) to examine and probe the structure of matter. In many ways the history of modern chemical instruments begins with the microscope.

MICROSCOPES: MOVING LIGHT

The microscope was invented by Antonie van Leeuwenhoek (1632–1723). The instrument is composed of a series of lenses that are used to magnify images. A lens is a curved piece of glass that focuses light rays and magnifies images in a microscope. The simplest lens used in forensic chemistry is a magnifying glass. This lens creates a false image on the retina in the eye that appears anywhere from four to 10 times as large as the real sample (4X–10X). This false image is also called a virtual image. Unlike the image produced from a movie projector, a virtual image does not actually exist in a place in space. When the magnifying glass is moved away from the sample, the image disappears; it only exists when one is looking directly through the lens.

Aside from virtual images, there are lenses that create real images such as those projected on a movie screen. When light from the projector passes through the front lens, a larger real image is projected into the theater and focuses on the distant screen. Unlike the virtual image, a real image exists no matter where the viewer is, and it does not depend on the person looking through a special lens. Both real and virtual images are used in a microscope.

A microscope is an optical system that focuses an intense light through a tiny sample and through a series of lenses to create a highly magnified image of the sample in the viewer's eye. Light originates from an intense bulb and is focused onto a mirror that directs it into the condenser, which compresses the rays into a bright cone of light directed through the sample. This design is called transmitted light because the light moves through the sample. Another form of microscopy relies on reflected light, which is used when samples are too thick to allow light through.

Once the light has passed through the sample, it is collected by the objective lens (the one nearest to the sample), which adds the first magnification. Most microscopes have a series of objective lenses ranging from 10X to 100X. The image is magnified again by the ocular, or eyepiece, lens, which is usually 4X or 10X. If the eyepiece is 4X and

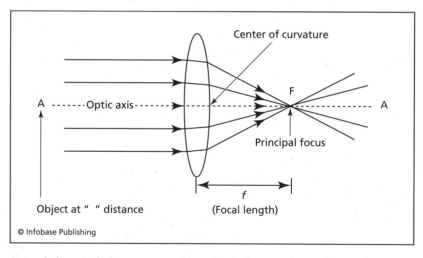

© Infobase Publishing

A simple lens. As light passes an object that is far away from a lens and enters the lens, the light rays are bent. They converge or focus at the point called the principal focus. The imaginary line running down the center of the lens is called the optic axis.

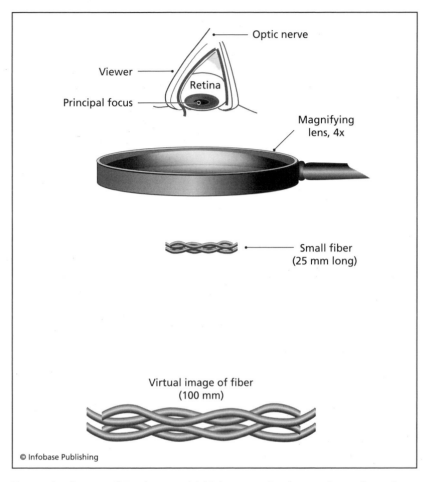

Optic nerve

Viewer

Retina

Principal focus

Magnifying lens, 4x

Small fiber (25 mm long)

Virtual image of fiber (100 mm)

© Infobase Publishing

How a simple magnifying lens works. Light passes by the specimen through the lens and creates a magnified image inside the eye that appears much larger than the real sample. This larger image, which is not real, is called the virtual image.

the objective lens in place 100X, total magnification of the sample is 400X.

Forensic chemists use microscopes to study crystals, examine samples, and perform microchemistry experiments and measurements. Many simple qualitative and quantitative tests that are performed using large equipment can be done with the microscope. This is often

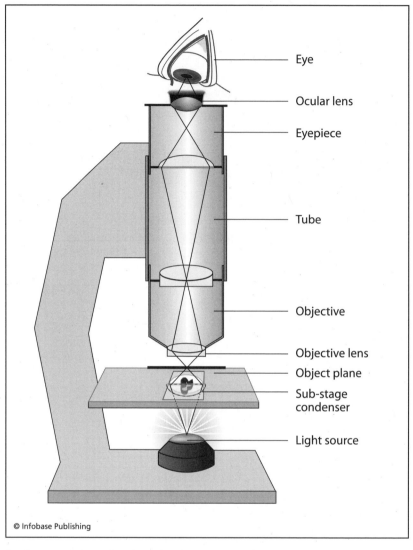

Eye

Ocular lens

Eyepiece

Tube

Objective

Objective lens

Object plane

Sub-stage condenser

Light source

© Infobase Publishing

A microscope. A modern biological or compound microscope contains a series of lenses. Light passing upward through the sample is called transmitted light. The drawing shows where the lenses create virtual and real images.

important because forensic scientists must conserve as much of a sample as possible. Fibers, hairs, and soils are also studied microscopically. One of the most useful developments in the past 15 years has been the marriage of microscopes with other chemical instruments.

Walter McCrone and Microchemistry

At first it might seem as if history, forensic chemistry, and microscopes have little in common. Nothing could be further from the truth. Many chemical tests used as part of forensic chemistry and toxicology can be performed on a small scale, so small that the results require the use of a microscope to observe. Specialized tests and analyses using microscopes have also been developed and used. The man most responsible for the modern marriage of chemistry and microscopy is Dr. Walter McCrone (1916–2002).

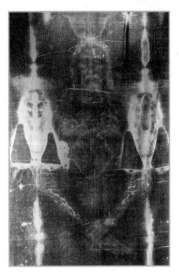

Negative head and torso views of the Shroud of Turin, dated May 18, 2006 (© P Deliss/Godong/Corbis)

McCrone was well known for his microscopic detective work in famous cases such as the Shroud of Turin. The shroud was a sacred relic of the Catholic Church believed by many to be the burial cloth of Jesus. The image of a man, arms crossed and eyes closed, looks much as one would expect the body to look after crucifixion. In 1978 a scientific team that included McCrone was given access to the shroud to perform tests. McCrone used tape to collect samples from the linen cloth for microscopic examination. He studied the particles adhering to the tape and discovered particles of pigments and collagen, a material used as the binding media in many paint formulas. McCrone provided strong evidence the Shroud of Turin is a painting created with very dilute paints, much like modern watercolors. The finding was controversial but was supported by later scientific analyses that used carbon dating techniques to date the linen used in the shroud to the early 1300s. He worked on many other art forgery cases, but none brought the same attention as did the Shroud of Turin.

HYPHENATED INSTRUMENTS: SEPARATION AND DETECTION

Aside from microscopes, forensic chemists rely on analytical instruments. Development of modern chemical instruments began in the late 1800s and accelerated dramatically around 1940. The most important classes of instruments in forensic chemistry are spectrophotometers and those that use "hyphenated" techniques. A hyphenated instrument has two modules that are linked together in one unit. The first module is a separation module, while the second is a detector. These two aspects were mentioned earlier as part of spot tests and TLC. The difference here is that the process now takes place inside a modular instrumental system. A sample that contains more than one component can be introduced into the first module, where it will be separated into individual components, much as in TLC. In an instrument, however, flow continues to move, pushing components one at a time into the detector. This separation is essential because most detectors cannot distinguish between different compounds.

The most commonly used hyphenated instrument in forensic chemistry is a gas chromatograph–mass spectrometer (GC-MS). A GC works similarly to TLC except hot gases are the solvent (the mobile phase) and the solid material (solid phase) is coated on the inside of a GC column. The column is long and thin with a diameter smaller than a piece of thin spaghetti. The solid material is coated in a layer that is too thin to see, and most of the inside of the column is empty space, like a tiny pipe with a thin layer of paint on the inside. The sample molecules can stay in the gas and move quickly through the pipe, or they may stick in the solid phase (the paint) and move more slowly. The molecules that tend to stick to the solid coating will come out of the column later than materials that prefer the fast-moving gas. Because GC is an effective means of separation, complex mixtures can be introduced into the instrument. This means that sample preparation does not have to be long and involved, which is a significant advantage.

Another type of hyphenated instrument is the gas chromatograph–flame ionization detector (GC-FID). In FID the detector is sensitive to the compounds found in gasoline, kerosene, and many other substances. The GC-FID is used for the analysis of arson cases. Finally, some labs use a high-pressure liquid chromatograph (HPLC) as a separation module

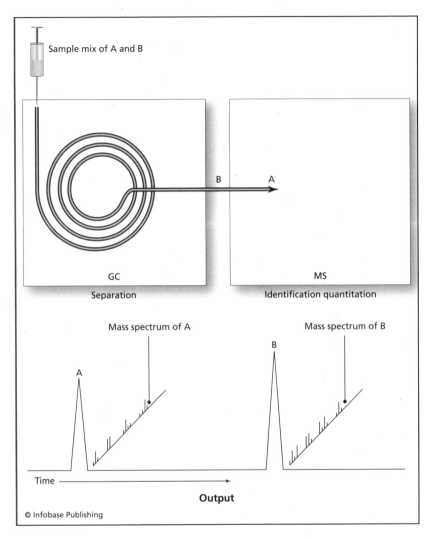

Gas chromatograph–mass spectrometer (GC-MS). This instrument has two modules. The GC component employs partitioning to separate a complex mixture into the individual components A and B. A comes out of the GC first and enters the MS, with B emerging a few seconds or minutes later. The mass spectrum is used to identify the compound and, in some cases, to perform quantitative analysis. The detector (the MS) sees each compound alone, so it is much easier to identify.

coupled to spectroscopic detectors or to mass spectrometers. Even DNA analysis uses hyphenated chemical instruments to separate the DNA pieces and then detect the pieces using a specialized detector. Like so many forensic instruments, this detector is based on the principles of spectrophotometry.

SPECTROPHOTOMETRY: INSTRUMENTS AND ELECTROMAGNETIC ENERGY

Spectrophotometry (also called spectroscopy) is the study of the interaction of electromagnetic energy with matter. Electromagnetic energy can be described as a wave. Think of a rock dropped into water. Waves emanate from the rock and propagate outward through the water. The waves are not new matter added from the rock, only ripples in the water caused by the rock.

The energy of waves is related to their wavelength and frequency. The wavelength is the distance from one wave crest to the next. In the visible range of the spectrum (energy that humans detect as colors), the wavelength is between 400 and 700 nanometers (1 nanometer [nm] equals 1 one-billionth of a meter). The frequency of energy is the number of waves that pass a fixed point per second. In the rock and water example a person standing on the shore could count how many waves hit the shoreline per second, which would be the frequency of the waves. Radios are calibrated in frequency, so a radio station picked up at the setting 95.5 would be broadcasting energy waves with a frequency of 95.5 kHz, or 95.5 million waves arriving per second. The hertz (Hz) is a measure of frequency, with 1 Hz equaling one wave per second. If in the rock in the pond example five waves hit the shore each second, the frequency of the waves would be 5 Hz. Wavelength and frequency are related by the equation $c = \lambda v$, which states that the speed of light (3×10^8 m/sec.) equals the frequency of a given wave times its wavelength.

There are spectrophotometers that work in all ranges of the electromagnetic spectrum. The first developed was based on colorimetry, in which the visible portion of electromagnetic energy is used. A colorimeter is useful for analyzing color, which might seem unnecessary, but color can be an important characteristic of forensic evidence, such as the results of color tests or the color of paints, hair, ink, or fibers. People perceive color in different ways, but an instrument only measures characteristics. An instrument can also often detect subtle differences in color that the human eye cannot. Variations of colorimetry are used forensically in the analysis of drugs, paint, and fibers.

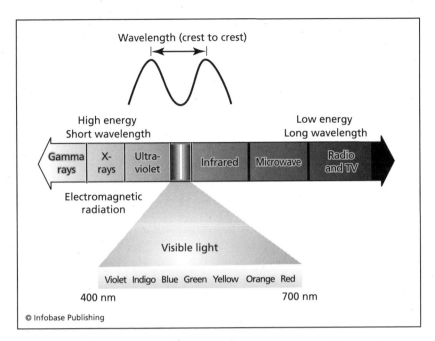

Wavelength (crest to crest)

High energy
Short wavelength

Low energy
Long wavelength

Gamma rays | X-rays | Ultra-violet | | Infrared | Microwave | Radio and TV

Electromagnetic radiation

Visible light

Violet Indigo Blue Green Yellow Orange Red

400 nm   700 nm

© Infobase Publishing

The electromagnetic spectrum. The highest energy waves are X-rays and cosmic rays, which have short wavelengths and high frequency. At the opposite end of the spectrum are television waves, with long wavelengths and low frequency. The visible portion is the only part humans can sense directly, and it incorporates the colors of the rainbow. When combined, these appear white.

All spectrometers consist of an energy (light) source, a mechanism or device to filter the source energy and select the wavelength(s) of interest, a device or method to hold the sample, and a detector system, which converts electromagnetic energy (light) to a measurable electrical current. The way in which energy is absorbed reveals information about the chemistry of the materials that are absorbing it. Spectrophotometers that work in the X-ray range of the electromagnetic spectrum, for example, are used to identify metals such as lead and antimony that are part of gunshot residues. On the other hand, the ultraviolet-visible (UV-Vis) range is useful for inks, paints, and drugs.

The most versatile form of spectrophotometry used in forensic chemistry is infrared (IR) spectroscopy. IR spectroscopy is used in drug analysis, toxicology, and in the analysis of inks, paints, fibers, papers, tapes, and many other types of physical evidence. Humans can sense

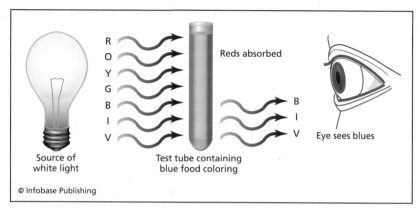

Colorimetry. In this style of spectrophotometry the eye is the detector, the energy is sunlight, and the matter is a test tube with some blue food coloring. Visible light can be broken into the colors of the rainbow: red, orange, yellow, blue, indigo, and violet. When the sun or a lightbulb shines through the test tube, the molecules that make up the food coloring absorb most of the red, yellow, and orange light. This leaves the blue light free to travel through the solution to the eye, where nerve cells fire and are interpreted by the brain as "blue."

IR indirectly as heat because it is related to the motion of molecules. The more molecules move, the more energy they have and the more energy they can donate in a collision. This is a complicated way of saying "do not put your hand on a hot stove." The stove feels hot because the molecules in the burner are moving very quickly. Temperature is an expression of the relative speed and motion of molecules. Motion can be translational (going from one place to another), rotational, or vibrational (shaking and wiggling). IR spectroscopy is based on vibrational motion.

When molecules absorb IR energy, it causes them to vibrate. To visualize this, atoms within a molecule can be thought of as tiny steel marbles and the chemical bonds connecting them as springs. Absorption of the IR radiation causes the spring to flex and bend, but the energy is not sufficient to break the spring. Since the molecular motion is three dimensional, there are many different types of motion that can occur, as shown in the figure. Because each bond between two different atoms has many different possible motions and because molecules are composed of many such atoms and bonds, the IR absorption pattern for any one molecule is unique.

To produce an IR spectrum of a sample, it is placed in the IR spectrophotometer such that it is exposed to different wavelengths of IR energy. Some of these wavelengths will be absorbed, causing the water molecule to vibrate as just described. Other wavelengths will pass through the water without being absorbed. A detector records the results, and a plot is made of the degree of absorbance at each wavelength. The resulting plot is called the IR spectrum of that sample. Most IR spectra are complex, but that complexity allows for identification. IR spectrophotometry is an important technique for forensic chemists who work in drug analysis.

Many spectrophotometric techniques are based not on the absorption of energy but on the emission. Inductively coupled plasma atomic

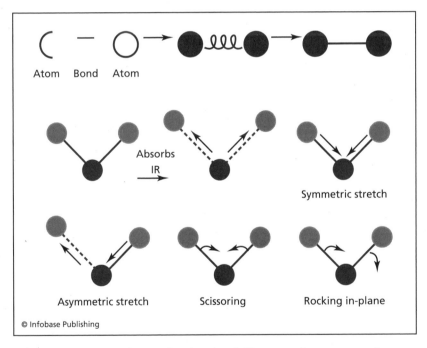

© Infobase Publishing

Infrared (IR) motion. When molecules absorb IR energy, they can move in different ways. This motion is what humans measure as temperature and call "heat"—the more motion, the hotter the temperature.

emission spectroscopy (ICP-AES) relies on the emission of character-istic wavelengths of light for elemental analysis. Fluorescence methods exploit the absorption of energy, typically in the ultraviolet range, to pro-duce emissions that reveal information about the element or compound.

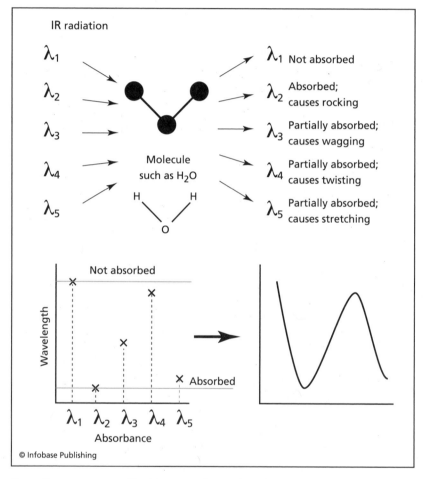

© Infobase Publishing

Recording a spectrum. The IR energy directed at the sample is absorbed in different ways that are characteristic of the molecule. A plot of the amount of energy absorbed at each IR wavelength is called the IR spectrum.

(Opposite) Sample IR spectra. The wavelength of IR energy is changing across the X axis, and the deeper the "valley" in the spectrum, the more strongly the IR energy is absorbed. The spectra look complex, but this complexity allows forensic chemists to distinguish the three molecules.

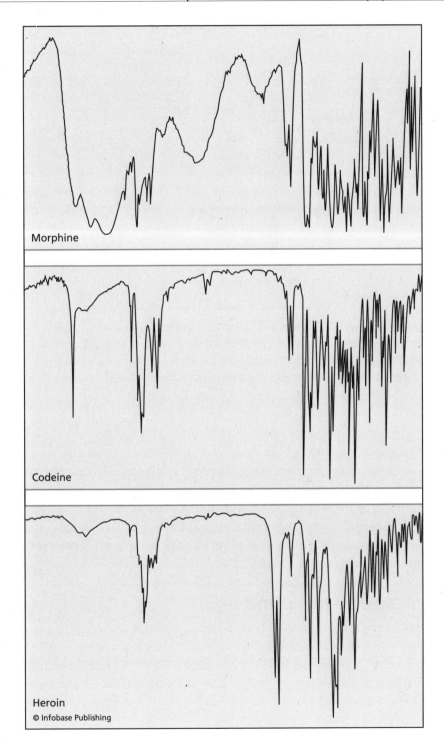

Morphine

Codeine

Heroin

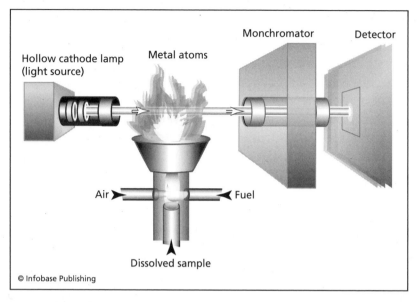

Atomic absorption spectroscopy (AAS). The sample is dissolved in an acid and drawn into a flame, which frees the metal atoms, such as lead, from the solution. The atoms absorb energy from the lamp, and the more atoms of a given metal that are present, the more energy absorbed. Each element requires a different lamp.

Examples include X-ray fluorescence (XRF) and spectrofluorometry. Spectrophotometers can also be used as the detector module in hyphenated instruments, but these are not as common in forensic chemistry as are GC-MS instruments. Finally, an instrument called an atomic absorption spectrophotometer (AAS) is used in forensic science to detect and give quantitative results for metals such as lead, mercury, arsenic, and antimony. Many of these metals are poisonous, so the instrument is particularly useful in toxicology.

MICROSPECTROPHOTOMETRY

Forensic chemists have recently added a powerful technique to their toolboxes, one that combines a microscope with a spectrophotometer to create a microspectrophotometer (MSP). This is a natural marriage because a microscope is designed to focus light through a sample, and spectrometry studies the interaction of energy with matter. The

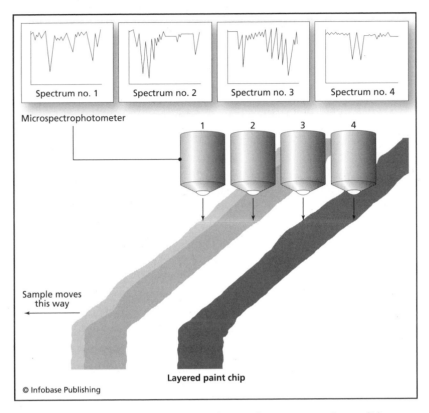

Depiction of surface mapping. A layered paint chip is mounted on a slide and placed on the stage of a microspectrophotometer (MSP). A spectrum is obtained from the first layer and then the stage is moved to the left for the next spectrum. Because each paint layer is chemically different, each spectrum in the map will show these differences.

most difficult aspect of designing MSPs is making sure that enough electromagnetic energy flows through the sample to get a meaningful interaction and a useful spectrum. The breakthrough came with the development of detectors so sensitive that they have to be cooled in liquid nitrogen to make sure that normal electrical and background noise does not drown out the tiny signal produced by the MSP. An MSP instrument consists of a microscope and lenses, as described above, but the lenses and other materials must consist of material that will not interfere with the measurements. For example, glass is a good absorber of IR energy. Because of this, the lenses in an MSP that works with IR energy cannot be made of glass. If they were all the IR energy would be absorbed by the lenses and never detected. It would be like building a microscope for looking at small specimens and making the lenses out of wood.

MSPs can be used in the X-ray, UV-Vis, and IR portions of the electromagnetic spectrum. Forensic chemists use them to study tiny paint chips, tapes, fibers, paper, coatings, plastic, and many other types of material. Combining the instrument with a motorized stage allows for surface mapping. To create a surface map of a fiber or other evidence the instrument focuses on a tiny portion of the sample, takes a spectrum, and then moves to the next point. This method is very useful for studying samples that are not the same throughout, such as a layered paint chip.

IMMUNOLOGICAL METHODS IN TOXICOLOGY

In addition to the techniques and instruments already described, toxicologists have another procedure useful for testing blood, urine, and other bodily fluid samples. This technique is called immunoassay, and there are several variations. Immunoassay relies on an antigen-antibody reaction between the drug being tested and an antibody specific for it. This is the same general kind of reaction that occurs when someone catches a cold; the body manufactures antibodies that attack the cold virus (the antigen). For immunoassay the antibody is attached to a solid surface, such as the bottom of a plastic or glass well. A complex that consists of the drug coupled to a label is then added to the container. The label is something that can be detected; for example, a radioactive tag would be detectable using a radiation detector, while a fluorescent label would be detected by light that it emits.

When this complex of drug and label is added to the container, a reaction occurs. As a result the labeled drug is bound to the antibody. A sample that may contain the drug, such as urine, is next added to the plastic well. If there is no or little drug present, the labeled drug-antibody complex will remain undisturbed. If there is a large concentration of the drug, this will displace the labeled drug from the antibodies, releasing the labeled drug into solution. The higher the drug concentration in

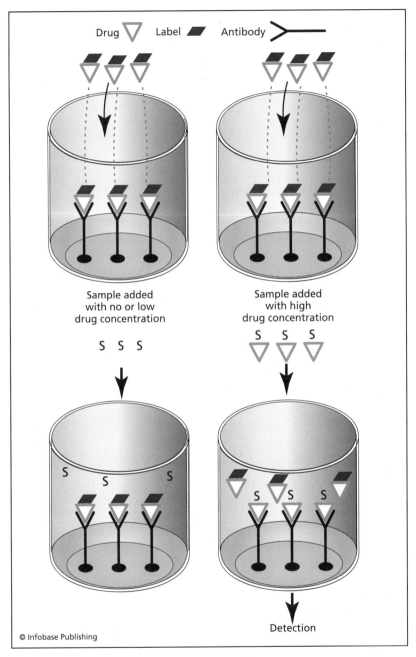

A simplified depiction of an immunoassay

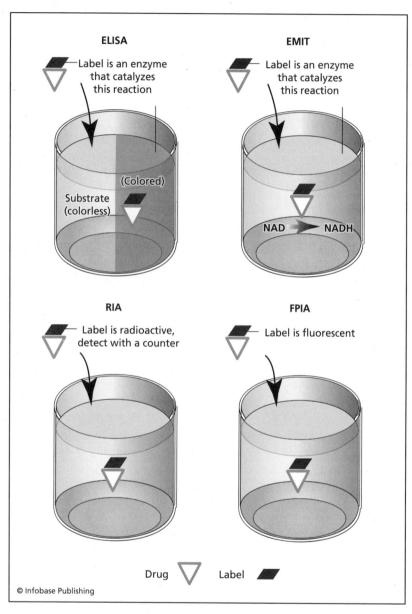

How the different methods of immunoassay work

the urine sample, the greater the displacement of the labeled drug. The amount of the displaced labeled drug is then measured.

The type of label used determines the type of immunoassay technique. In an enzyme-linked immunoassay (ELISA), a chemical compound called a substrate is added to the solution in the well. The label is an enzyme that catalyzes a reaction in which the substrate is changed, forming a colored solution. The deeper the color, the greater the concentration of the enzyme label present, which implies a greater concentration of drug in the original sample. The enzyme-multiplied immunoassay technique (EMIT) is similar; the label catalyzes a common biological reaction, the conversion of nicotinamide adenine dinucleotide (NAD) to a reduced form of the same molecule called NADH. The more NADH detected, the greater the concentration of drug in the sample. A radioimmunoassay (RIA) uses a radioactive label that can be detected by counting equipment. Finally, a fluorescent polarization immunoassay (FPIA) uses a fluorescent label and the directions in which the fluorescence is emitted.

3

Toxicology: Drugs and Poisons in the Body

"Only remember one thing—a small dose is a remedy, a large one is poison. One drop will restore life, as you have seen; five or six will inevitably kill, and in a way the more terrible inasmuch as, poured into a glass of wine, it would not in the slightest degree affect its flavor."

—The Count in *The Count of Monte Cristo*

What is a drug, what is a poison, and how are they differentiated? Often it is not the substance itself that makes something a drug or a poison but rather the amount of it that is ingested. The source of the substance does not matter; hemlock extracted from a plant is a deadly poison even though it could be regarded as an herbal tea. Many drugs are obtained from plants directly or were synthesized. Heavy-metal poisons such as lead can come from soil, batteries, or pollution. But no matter where a substance comes from, it is the dose that makes it a poison. Even common materials and pharmaceuticals can be poisons if too much is ingested.

The chemical structure of aspirin (acetylsalicylic acid)

A drug is a substance or compound that is used to treat or prevent a disease or to treat symptoms of a disease or injury. Aspirin (acetylsalicylic acid) is a drug that can be used to help prevent heart attacks or to treat the pain and swelling that results from an injury such as a twisted ankle. Strictly speaking, a drug is a single compound, while a mixture of compounds is defined as a medicine. Over-the-counter (OTC) cold medicines contain many substances, such as aspirin, decongestants, and antihistamines. Many people, however, use the terms *drug* and *medicine* interchangeably.

A drug acts to change the chemistry and conditions of the body; this is called the mechanism of action (MOA). Aspirin works by inhibiting the action of a class of compounds called prostaglandins, which promote many functions in the body. This explains in part why aspirin can be used to treat such variety of symptoms and conditions.

The history of aspirin as a drug is typical of many other substances, starting with folk knowledge. As early as 400 B.C.E. the Greek physician Hippocrates recommended that his patients chew on willow bark when they had a fever or pain. (Willow bark, as it turns out, contains compounds related to aspirin.) It is likely that the use of aspirin-based folk remedies predates this, perhaps by centuries, yet it took nearly 2,000 years for chemists to synthesize the active ingredient of aspirin. By the 1800s salicylic acid, which is closely related to acetylsalicylic acid and also found in willow bark, was available, but it produced stomach pain, a side effect still associated with aspirin. A German chemist, Felix Hoffman, is generally credited with the first synthesis of acetylsalicylic acid. Hoffman performed his work at a company with a familiar name, Bayer. Interestingly, Bayer, a company that has become nearly synonymous with aspirin, was not active in pharmaceuticals until the 1890s. Many of their early drugs were actually by-products of making dyes, a fairly complex chemical process and not as far removed from drug synthesis as it might seem. Aspirin hit the market in 1899 and soared in popularity. By 1915 it was available OTC so that anyone could purchase and use it. Still, it was not until the 1970s that scientists had unraveled the mechanism of the drug. Although aspirin was originally released as an analgesic (a drug meant to alleviate pain), many people who now take aspirin do so to prevent heart attack or for related reasons.

As useful as it has proven to be, aspirin is not without dangers and side effects. Some people are allergic to aspirin, and taking it can cause a deadly episode of anaphylactic shock (a severe immune response). Buffering aspirin can reduce stomach pain, but for many people stomach discomfort is part of taking an aspirin. An aspirin overdose can cause injury and death. Although aspirin is a drug, it is also a poison, which brings us back to the idea that "the dose makes the poison."

How then do a drug and a poison differ? A poison is a substance that is capable of causing harm to an organism, whether it is an illness, injury, or death. The modern definition of the term *poison* is essentially the same as that of a toxic substance. The more toxic or poisonous a substance is, the more harm a small amount of it can cause. Looking at it this way, everything is poisonous; it is the amount and time over which the substance is administered that determines how harmful it will be.

MEASURING TOXICITY

Although there are many measures of toxicity, one that is commonly used is the LD_{50} value, or lethal dose 50 percent. This is the dose that will result in the death of half of a test population that is exposed to this level of the substance in a single dose. A test population would be something such as a group of laboratory mice used in the experiment. A corollary to the LD_{50} is the ED_{50}, or effective dose 50 percent, which reflects the dose of a drug or medicine that shows a therapeutic effect in 50 percent of the tested patients. There are two graphical ways to interpret LD_{50} and ED_{50}. In both approaches the X axis is the dose, increasing from left to right. In the first approach (top frame of the figure), as the dose increases, it reaches a threshold at which some individuals taking that amount die.

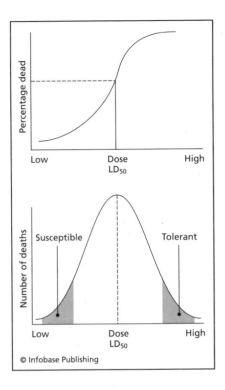

Graphical presentation of lethal and effective doses. In the top frame, the Y axis is the percentage of the population that dies at a given dose. At low doses only susceptible members of the population will die. Similarly, even at high doses, some will survive and are labeled as tolerant. The dose at which half of the population is affected is the 50th percentile. At the LD_{50} dose half of the test population dies. The bottom frame shows the same thing in a different way; the number of deaths peaks at the LD_{50}. The same methods can be used to evaluate effective dose.

These people (or test animals) are labeled "sensitive" or "susceptible," since they are affected at a lower dose than most. As the dose increases, the percentage of the test population that dies increases. A dose that kills 50 percent of the population is the LD_{50} value. There will be some individuals who are resistant or tolerant of that dose, and they will die only when ingesting more than the LD_{50}. A second graphical approach (bottom frame of the figure) shows what fraction of the population dies at a given dose, with the largest percentage dying at doses at or near the LD_{50}. For ED_{50} the graphs would be identical except that the effect noted would not be death but rather a therapeutic response to the drug. Some people would need smaller doses (susceptible) while others would need a larger dose (tolerant) to achieve the desired effect.

To find the LD_{50} toxicologists often turn to a document called the materials safety data sheet (MSDS) or other toxicity indexes found in books or online. An MSDS contains a wealth of information in addition to toxicity data, including how materials should be safely handled, stored, and disposed of. The following table shows a sampling of the toxicity data taken from the MSDS forms for two common household substances.

Which is more toxic? Acetylsalicylic acid (aspirin) can cause harm, at least in rats, at a lower dose than sodium chloride (table salt) can, but the data is incomplete. LD_{50} data will only be available if a substantially sized population is exposed to a substance. The data for rats is obtained from laboratory studies, but any human data has to come from accidental exposures. Children are much more likely to take a large dose of aspirin accidentally than are adults, and therefore, there is enough clinical data from such incidents to report a reliable LD_{50} value. The same is not true of table salt, for which rat data alone is presented. If the response of rats can be applied to humans, aspirin is more toxic than table salt.

For the sake of an example, assume that the LD_{50} for aspirin for an adult is 200 mg/kg, which refers to the amount of material in milligrams (mg) that is ingested per kilogram (kg) of body weight. A kilogram is the equivalent of 2.2 pounds, so a person's weight in kilograms will always be less than when the weight is expressed in pounds. To determine the LD_{50} value for a typical woman weighing 130 pounds the necessary calculations are

1. Convert her weight to kilograms.

$$130 \text{ lbs.} \times 1 \text{ lb} / 2.2 \text{ kg} = 59.1 \text{ kg}$$

1. Multiply her weight in kilograms by the LD_{50} value.

$$59.1 \text{ kg} \times 200 \text{ mg/kg} = 11,820 \text{ mg} = 11.8 \text{ g}$$

LETHAL DOSES OF COMMON MATERIALS TAKEN BY MOUTH (ORALLY)

LD_{50} (mg/kg)	acetylsalicylic acid (aspirin)	Sodium chloride (table salt)
oral child	104	not available
oral rat	200	3,000

For this 130-pound woman the LD_{50} value is almost 12 grams (g), nearly half of an ounce. A typical aspirin tablet contains 325 mg (1 milligram = 1/1000 of a gram) of aspirin, so this lethal dose translates to about 37 aspirin tablets. Does this mean that any woman weighing 130 pounds

The Most Toxic Substance?

Everything from dioxin (an environmental contaminant) to plutonium (a synthetic radioactive element) has been called the most toxic material ever known or made. Looking at the LD_{50} alone and ignoring for the moment that some people will be tolerant and some susceptible, the substance generally considered most toxic is the botulinum toxin. This toxin causes the disease called botulism, or botulism poisoning, and it has an LD_{50} of 0.00001 mg/kg, meaning that one gram of this substance would be enough (using simple assumptions and calculations) to kill roughly a million adult men.

The toxin itself is a protein produced by the bacteria *Clostridium botulinum*. The bacteria is anaerobic, meaning that it cannot survive in the presence of oxygen. Botulism poisoning can result from ingesting canned food that is infected with the bacteria. Such cans often have a bloated, bulging appearance. Once infected food is swallowed, the toxin is rapidly absorbed into the bloodstream. It acts as a neurotoxin, meaning that it attacks nerve function. In this case the toxin prevents the release of the neurotransmitter called acetylcholine. As a result one of the symptoms of botulism poisoning can be paralysis, as the muscles are unable to contract without the acetylcholine being present to transmit the signal down the nervous system. Often death occurs because the muscles used to breathe are paralyzed. Other symptoms, which appear within a few hours of ingestion, include nausea, vomiting, headache, weakness, and blurred vision. An antitoxin has been developed for botulism that can counteract the deadly paralysis, but survival usually depends on an early diagnosis and aggressive treatment to keep the patient breathing and nourished while treatments and time are allowed to work.

who swallows 37 aspirin tablets all at once will die? No, the LD_{50} is an average across a population, and as such, susceptible women would die taking fewer, while tolerant women could take more and survive. Even with these considerations the LD_{50} provides a quantitative measure of potential harm that is invaluable to a toxicologist. It allows scientists to compare the relative toxicity, on average, of materials such as table salt and aspirin.

If the same calculations are performed for the table salt, the LD_{50} for an average woman comes out to be about 178 g, approximately 15 times as much as the lethal dose calculated for aspirin. This amount of salt (178 g) is equivalent to a little more than six ounces, well in excess of the contents of a typical salt shaker, or about a quarter of the familiar round boxes that salt is sold in. Because saltwater induces vomiting, it is hard to imagine anyone being able to swallow this much salt without throwing up, making it very difficult to ingest enough at one sitting to die.

Although both aspirin and salt are toxic, the harmful dosage of each is high, and the danger is minimal. In fact, most people would not even identify salt or aspirin as poisonous. For comparison, the LD_{50} for a highly poisonous material such as potassium cyanide (KCN) is on the order of approximately 1 mg/kg of body weight, which translates to 59 mg for the hypothetical woman weighing 130 pounds. A baby aspirin tablet weighs 80 mg. A fatal dose of arsenic trioxide (AsO_3), a famous poison from ancient to Victorian times, would be about 106 mg. One of the most toxic substances known, the botulinum toxin, has an LD_{50} of 0.00001 mg/kg, or 0.59 microgram (μg; a microgram is 1 one-millionth of a gram), a speck of material far too small to see without the aid of a powerful microscope.

OTHER FACTORS IN TOXICITY

The amount of poison (the dose) is just one aspect of toxicity. There are other factors that must be considered when trying to determine how toxic a substance is to the person ingesting it. These include the following:

- size of the person
- inherent toxicity of the substance

- method (mode) of ingestion

- time over which the dose was administered

- rate of elimination compared with the rate of ingestion

- the person's health, age, and genetic factors

As shown with the earlier aspirin example, the size of the person ingesting the substance matters. Given that the material is distributed throughout the body once ingested, the smaller the person, the more concentrated the toxin will be in the blood or tissues. An analogy would be a tablespoon of sugar dissolved in a small teacup versus a large mug. Although it is the same amount of sugar, the tea in the teacup will taste much sweeter since it is dissolved in a smaller amount of tea than in the mug; thus, it is much more concentrated.

The inherent toxicity depends on how a drug or poison works, or its MOA. In general, the more toxic a substance is, the more critical the bodily process it attacks. The botulinum toxin is a potent neurotoxin, meaning that its mechanism is to attack the nervous system. Specifically, it impedes the release of a neurotransmitter resulting in the inability of neurons to transmit signals. As a result some of the symptoms of botulism poisoning include weakness of the muscles and paralysis, starting with eye muscles. Interestingly, tiny doses of the toxin are now used for cosmetic reasons because of these effects. Injection of the toxin into facial muscles can counteract wrinkling. This is known as the Botox injection procedure. Thus, even a substance called the "most toxic" has practical uses.

Carbon monoxide (CO), a toxic gas that results in many accidental poisonings each year, works by a different mechanism. It binds to hemoglobin in the blood much more strongly than oxygen does. As more CO is inhaled, more oxygen is displaced from the blood. Death can occur when about 50 percent of the oxygen has been displaced; death occurs as a result of suffocation (asphyxia, or lack of oxygen). The effects of CO poisoning are reversible if the poisoned person is given pure oxygen. The mechanisms of toxicity of CO and botulinum are completely different and lead to different inherent toxicities for these two substances.

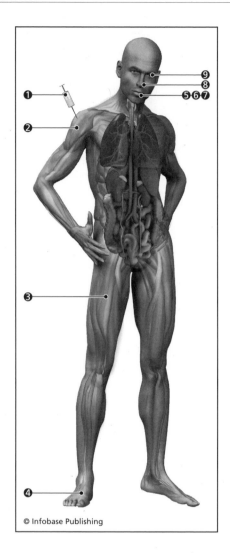

There are many ways for drugs and poisons to enter the body (see table, page 59)

© Infobase Publishing

There are many ways in which a toxic substance can be introduced into the body. Ingestion by mouth (swallowing) has been assumed so far, but it is only one of several ways by which a toxic substance can enter the body. While some seem odd ways to be poisoned, all are common ways in which drugs and medicines are administered. A new flu vaccine, for example, can be administered via a nasal inhaler. The mode of ingestion can influence how quickly an effect is observed. Direct injection of a substance into a vein can result in an almost immediate response

MODES OF INGESTION

Number (as indicated in figure)	Mode
1.	Injection into the tissue under the skin
2.	Injection into a vein (intravenous)
3.	Absorption through the skin (dermal)
4.	Injection into a muscle
5.	Inhalation of a gas or aspiration (inhalation of liquid)
6.	Ingestion into the stomach (oral)
7.	Dissolution below the tongue (sublingual)
8.	Absorption through the mucous membranes of the nose (nasal)
9.	Absorption through the eyes

since the substance is rapidly distributed by the bloodstream to the body. Similarly, inhalation usually produces a faster response than ingestion into the stomach as the substance is delivered to the lungs where there is direct contact between the lung tissue and the blood system.

The time over which a substance is ingested is another critical factor in determining its toxicity. In the body an ingested material is subject to many processes. Once the substance is introduced, it is absorbed and distributed via the circulatory system throughout the body and to different organs, such as the liver, where metabolic processes occur. Metabolism changes the chemical form of the substance, creating new materials (metabolites) that follow the same path as the original. Water-soluble forms of the substance can be excreted in the urine, sweat, or tears, while gaseous by-products can be exhaled. Materials that are fat soluble or otherwise bound up in the body are retained, sometimes for years or a lifetime. If the original substance is water soluble, it is not unusual for some of it to be excreted in its original form.

How long this transformation and elimination scheme takes is critical in determining the toxicity of the substance. If the rate of elimination is fast, toxicity decreases, as even large doses can be removed relatively quickly. If the rate of elimination is slow, materials will build up, increasing the toxicity. Depending on the balance of the rate of ingestion versus

Absorbed Poisons

It is possible to absorb a fatal dose of a poison, even through protective gloves. Toxicologists played an important role in the investigation of the illness and death of Karen Wetterhahan, a professor in the Dartmouth College Department of Chemistry, in February 1997. Wetterhahan, 48, was using dimethyl mercury (CH_3-Hg-CH_3) in her research. As described in a report issued by the U.S. Occupational Health and Safety Administration (OSHA), the incident occurred while she was working in a fume hood and wearing latex gloves.

During the transfer of liquid from one container to another, she apparently spilled a small amount (a few drops at most) on the back of one of the gloves. Wetterhahan reported that she took off the gloves and gave the incident no further thought. Later studies proved that the organic liquid quickly and easily penetrated the latex examination gloves, delivering the lethal dose via skin absorption. The fume hood likely protected her from exposure from inhalation, which could have occurred given that dimethyl mercury evaporates relatively easily.

The first neurological symptoms appeared months later, when Wetterhahan reported numbness, tingling, and difficulty speaking. Given the symptoms and her area of research, her medical teams suspected mercury poisoning. The suspicion was confirmed by further testing, including hair analysis. Mercury levels were recorded at 234 ppb (parts per billion, or ug/L) in her urine and at 4,000 ppb in her blood months after the exposure. Despite therapy she died nearly 10 months after the incident. As a result of this accident chemists and researchers around the world were warned to use protective gloves other than latex when handling dimethyl mercury. Undoubtedly lives were saved. Had it not been for advances in forensic chemistry and toxicology, the cause of her death might never have been revealed.

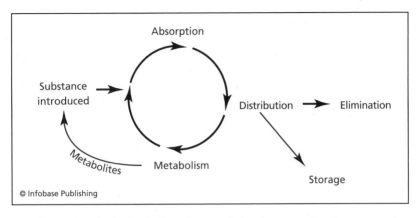

Absorption

Substance
introduced

Distribution → Elimination

Metabolites — Metabolism

Storage

© Infobase Publishing

Transformations in the body. Once ingested, the drug or poison is processed
by the body through metabolism.

the rate of elimination, a large dose may not produce toxic effects. Again,
consider the aspirin example. If the adult woman took an aspirin tablet
(325 mg) every day for a year to help prevent heart attacks, this would
correspond to a dose of 137 grams, more than 10 times the LD_{50} calculated above. Aspirin is eliminated quickly, however, and it is taken
in small doses over time. Thus, taking 137 grams in this way is not
dangerous.

Although simplified, this example illustrates the difference between
chronic exposure (longer times, lower amounts) and acute exposure
(higher doses, shorter times) to toxins. Forensic toxicologists more
often deal with acute poisoning, in which large amounts of the poison
are ingested at one sitting or over a brief period. However, chronic poisonings are not uncommon. Arsenic, the historical favorite, was usually administered in small doses over time, as it accumulates gradually.
In this way the symptoms appear incrementally and mimic those of
common diseases. Similarly, many environmental toxins are pollutants
found in small amounts in soil, air, and water. Arsenic is a trace pol-
lutant found in drinking water in the western United States as well
as in areas of Pakistan and Bangladesh. People who drink the water
will accumulate arsenic in their bodies and eventually exhibit the same
symptoms as those poisoned intentionally with arsenic powder. Other
examples of environmental toxins are DDT, dioxin, and metals such as
lead and mercury. These substances can occur as trace environmental

contaminants that build up in a person's system as a result of low-level, chronic exposure.

Other factors that define toxicity depend on the person who has ingested the material. Age can be critical, with children and the elderly generally being more susceptible to toxic effects than other age groups. General health is important, as are genetic effects. Some people are inherently sensitive to or tolerant of substances based on their genes. Thus, toxicity of a substance is the cumulative effect of a variety of factors.

PHARMACOKINETICS AND TOXICOKINETICS

Pharmacology is the study of how drugs (pharmaceuticals) are transformed in the body. Pharmacology can be roughly divided into two aspects: pharmacodynamics and pharmacokinetics. The term *dynamics* refers to movement or motion, while *kinetics* refers to speed or rate of movement. A simple distinction between the two terms is that pharmacodynamics focuses on the way a drug affects a person over time, while pharmacokinetics traces the route and rate of transformations of a drug once it is ingested.

Toxicologists are interested in pharmacokinetics because it provides a means of studying the concentrations of drugs and metabolites that may be found in blood and tissues as well as how a drug is metabolized and excreted over time. The term toxicokinetics is also sometimes used to describe the same phenomena when the substance ingested is toxic; it is considered a subdiscipline of pharmacokinetics. Elements of toxicokinetics include

- modes of ingestion

- rates of absorption and distribution

- biotransformations and their rates

- relative concentrations of drugs and metabolites in different tissues

- rates of elimination

All of these processes are important in determining what a toxicologist looks for in submitted samples. Additionally, understanding of the

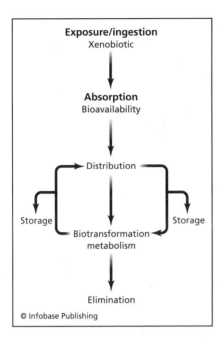

Exposure/ingestion
Xenobiotic

Absorption
Bioavailability

Distribution

Storage

Storage

Biotransformation
metabolism

Elimination

© Infobase Publishing

Simplified view of toxicokinetics. Once a drug or poison gets into the body, there are three stages that it passes through. First is absorption, such as in the stomach or through the lungs if the substance is a gas. Next, the bloodstream distributes the material. Finally, it is eliminated. The metabolism and elimination steps may take hours, days, or even longer.

toxicokinetics of a substance can help re-create events or answer such questions as how much of a drug or poison was taken and when.

When a toxic substance or drug is introduced into the body, three general processes occur. For any detectable concentration of the substance to be found in blood, it must first be absorbed into the bloodstream. How and where this occurs depends on the nature of the substance and on the mode of ingestion. As an example, consider the act of drinking a glass of wine, which typically would contain around 10 percent ethanol (ethyl alcohol). Ingestion occurs by swallowing, and absorption into the bloodstream occurs primarily in the small intestine. As absorption proceeds, blood concentration of ethanol increases, and ethanol is delivered to all tissues of the body, including the brain. This phase is referred to as distribution. Any toxic effects (or therapeutic effects in the case of a drug) will depend on a sufficient concentration of the substance reaching the target organ, site, or structure. In the case of ethanol, a water-soluble compound, it can be distributed throughout the body, favoring tissues that have the highest water content. Toxic effects (also called intoxication) can occur in any organ, and in the case of alcohol, these will be seen in the brain and liver. If the concentration becomes high enough in the brain, observable toxic effects will be seen, as alcohol is a central nervous system depressant. If concentrations continue to rise, drunkenness is the observable result. In the case of ethanol it takes about an hour for the maximum concentration to be reached in the blood.

Once a substance is distributed, bodily processes start to act on it and may result in the chemical conversion of some or all of the original substance into other compounds (metabolites). Collectively these transformations are called biotransformations, since they occur within a biological system. Operating concurrently with metabolism is the process of elimination, which removes a substance and its metabolites from the body. For the ethanol in the glass of wine, approximately 10 percent of it will pass unchanged into the urine, sweat, or breath. The remaining 90 percent is metabolized in the liver, where toxic effects

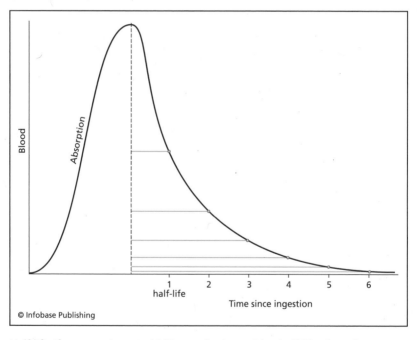

© Infobase Publishing

Half-life. If a person ingested 100 mg of a drug with a half-life of one hour, at the end of that hour, 50 mg of the unchanged drug would remain in his or her system. After two hours, 25 mg would remain, and so on. Half-life measures the persistence of a substance in the body.

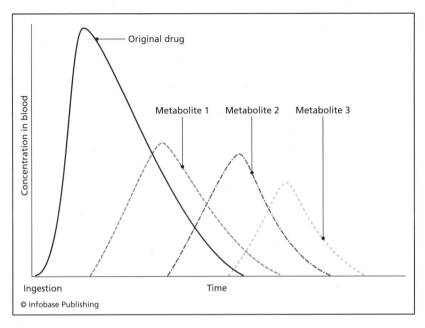

Multiple transformations. As the original drug breaks down according to its half-life, the concentration of the resulting metabolite increases. It, too, has a half-life and will degrade, forming another breakdown product, and so on.

can occur if a person has chronic exposure to alcohol. Eventually the alcohol is converted to carbon dioxide and water, but this process is relatively slow and can take hours, depending on how much alcohol was consumed. It also occurs in steps. For alcohol the first step is the conversion of ethanol (CH_3-CH_2OH) to acetaldehyde (CH_3-CHO). In the metabolic process some steps are fast, and some are relatively slow. The slowest step in any transformation is referred to as the rate-limiting step.

The rate of elimination or conversion of a substance can be expressed as its half-life ($t_{1/2}$). The half-life of a toxin is the time required to remove or transform one-half of the total available. In general it takes about 10 half-lives for the concentration of a substance to fall to the point that it is essentially gone. A metabolite of cocaine, for example, that has a half-life of a day in urine will become undetectable after about 10 days. The longer the half-life of a substance, the longer it will remain in a tissue or fluid. If the method of removal of a substance is conversion into another, such as the conversion of alcohol into acetaldehyde, then the cycle starts again, with the new substance undergoing absorption, distribution, and elimination, with the rate of elimination expressed by another half-life. When any substance is ingested, it initiates a complex series of related transformations and eliminations that can result in the final excretion of a substance that is entirely different from the original. With a glass of wine, most of the alcohol, which is water-soluble liquid, is eliminated after several steps, leading to exhalation of carbon dioxide, an insoluble gas.

TYPES OF SAMPLES AND ANALYSIS

The types of samples that a forensic toxicologist may be asked to analyze are principally blood, urine, and tissue samples. There are, however, many other samples that occasionally must be tested. As discussed in preceding sections, drugs and poisons are distributed to the body by the bloodstream, and where those substances or their metabolites concentrate depends on the drug, how it breaks down, half-lives, and other factors. Also important is the time elapsed since ingestion, given that materials will partition into different fluids and tissues over time. Toxicologists are also interested in the relative concentrations of materials in different samples. After a person drinks a glass of wine, for example, the concentration of alcohol will increase in the blood and then decrease as it is metabolized in the liver or excreted unchanged. The difference between the concentration of the alcohol in the blood and the urine can be used to backtrack to an estimated time of ingestion.

Other drugs, like cocaine, and poisons, such as arsenic, can leave traces elsewhere, as in the saliva and even in the hair. Hair can be particularly useful, providing a permanent record of ingestion for some drugs and toxins. Hair grows from the root, and once the hair has grown slightly away from the root, it is isolated from blood flow and further metabolic changes. While in contact with the blood at the root, substances can be trapped in the hair and then frozen in place there. As hair grows, that section moves away from the root at a steady rate. By cutting a length of hair and analyzing it in sections it is sometimes possible to find drugs, poisons, and their metabolites and to estimate when the dose was taken.

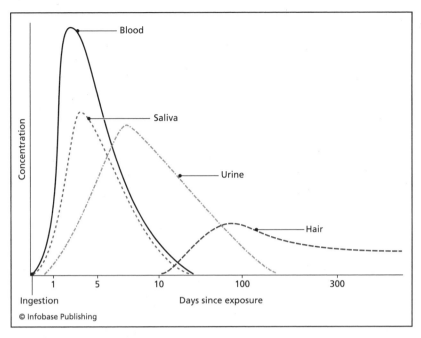

Relative concentrations. After a substance is ingested and distributed, its
concentration in the blood will start to fall as concentrations in other body
"compartments" increase.

AREAS OF FORENSIC TOXICOLOGY

Forensic toxicologists are trained not only in sample analysis but also
in the complex processes of ingestion and its modes: biotransformation
and metabolism, absorption, and elimination. This knowledge allows
toxicologists to re-create the original ingestion in much the same way
the analysis of physical evidence allows forensic scientists to re-create
the events at a crime scene. But before there can be re-creation, there
must be analysis.

For most forensic toxicology analyses the first test performed is an
immunoassay screening or combination of screenings. Immunoassay
results will narrow down what may be present, but alone the results are
inconclusive and will require more work. TLC may also be used. The
next step is usually an instrumental method, such as GC-MS, to confirm
the identity of compounds, find others not tested for in the immunoassay, and determine the concentrations of drugs and metabolites of

interest that are found. With this information the toxicologist can re-create what the person ingested and roughly when they ingested it. Very often there will be a mix of substances found, so the task of re-creating the ingestion event can be complex. Forensic toxicology can be roughly divided into these three areas: human performance toxicology, postmortem toxicology, and workplace toxicology.

Human performance toxicology refers primarily to alcohol intoxication. There are many kinds of alcohols, such as isopropanol (isopropyl alcohol, or rubbing alcohol) and methanol (wood alcohol). In the forensic lab the target alcohol is ethanol (ethyl alcohol). Ethanol is the type of alcohol found in beer, wine, liquors, and in some medications. In liquor, such as gin and vodka, the amount of ethanol is reported as its "proof." The proof of a sample is twice the percentage of ethanol it contains. Thus, an 86-proof whiskey would be 43 percent ethanol by volume. Wine is about 3–5 percent ethanol, but since wine is not classified as a hard liquor, the term *proof* does not apply.

The intoxication that results from ethanol depends on how much a person ingests over a given period of time, his or her size, the person's stomach contents, and other factors. The degree of intoxication is reported in terms of the blood alcohol concentration (BAC). The unit of BAC used in a legal setting is usually percentage by volume. In most states the legal limit is 0.08 percent, meaning that anyone whose blood has a concentration of alcohol that is 0.08 percent (0.08 g of ethanol per 100 ml of blood) or greater is considered to be legally intoxicated. There are noticeable effects at lower concentrations, however. At levels of approximately 0.03 percent, the person may feel euphoric and have impaired judgment. These effects increase with increasing intoxication. Once BAC levels approach 0.4 percent, coma can result, and levels of around 0.45 percent can result in death. According to the National Highway Transportation Safety Administration, intoxicated drivers kill about 18,000 people per year, roughly one death every 30 minutes. This does not include accidents involving other vehicles such as off-road vehicles, snowmobiles, trains, etc. Data from a 2001 survey (the latest available) reports that nearly a quarter of the drivers responding had driven within two hours of drinking alcohol. Approximately 1,400 college students die each year as a result of ethanol consumption. For a substance most people would consider nontoxic, alcohol kills an alarming number of people.

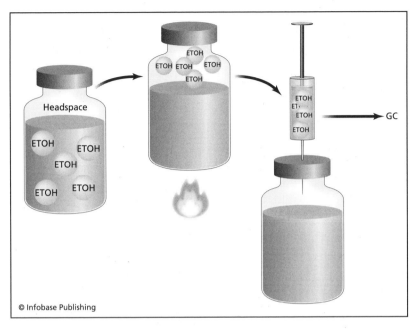

ETOH
ETOH ETOH ETOH
ETOH

Headspace

ETOH
ETOH
ETOH
ETOH ETOH

ETOH
ET·
ETOH
ETOH

GC

© Infobase Publishing

Laboratory analysis for alcohol in blood. Ethanol in the blood is driven into the headspace, which is sampled and tested.

The job of the toxicologist in these cases is to analyze the BAC. When the operator of a vehicle is suspected of being drunk, trained personnel draw a blood sample as soon as possible. Time is important because, as explained in the preceding sections, the concentration of the alcohol in the body is constantly changing. If too much time elapses between the incident and the taking of the blood sample, the BAC results will be less representative of intoxication at the time of the incident. A forensic toxicologist analyzes the blood sample, and the concentration of alcohol is reported as grams per deciliter or as a percentage of total blood volume, as described in the preceding section.

The analysis of ethanol is performed using a headspace sampling technique. The blood sample is placed in a small vial such that there is an empty portion (headspace) remaining. The vial is sealed and heated gently, which forces ethanol out of the blood and into the headspace. A small portion of the headspace is sampled and introduced into a gas chromatograph, which detects the ethanol. The data is used to calculate the BAC.

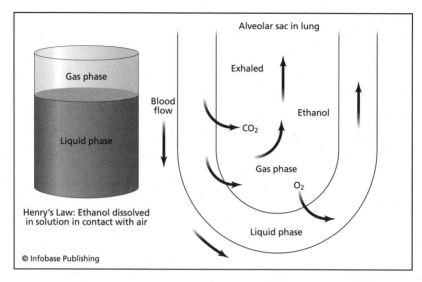

Breath alcohol. The concentration of ethanol in exhaled breath can be related to the concentration of ethanol in the blood through Henry's law.

Before a blood sample is taken, a police officer must first have reason to believe that a person is intoxicated. For example, the officer might observe someone driving erratically and stop them. Once the driver has been pulled over, the officer would perform tests that may include a breath alcohol test. This test does not provide the exact blood alcohol level, but it can provide enough information to determine if further action, such as drawing blood, is necessary.

Breath alcohol measurements rely on a relationship called Henry's law, which states that the concentration of a substance above a liquid is proportional to the concentration of that substance dissolved in the liquid. In this case the liquid is the blood flowing through the lungs in the areas where oxygen is taken in and carbon dioxide is expelled. Since ethanol evaporates easily, it will also move into the air at this interface. According to Henry's law, the concentration of ethanol in blood is about 2,100 times as high as the concentration in the air above it. Thus, measurement of the ethanol in someone's exhaled breath can be related to the concentration of ethanol in his or her blood. Small portable devices are used to measure breath alcohol in the field. Breath alcohol measurement is not as reliable as analyzing a blood sample, but the results are adequate to determine if there is probable cause to assume that someone is intoxicated.

Another area of human performance toxicology is in sports. This is not forensic toxicology in the traditional sense, since many of the drugs that scientists test in these cases are not illegal. In Olympic competition the World Anti-Doping Agency and the United States Anti-Doping Agency maintain lists of the banned substances, as do most professional sports organizations. The lists include illegal drugs, steroids, and substances that enhance the transportation of oxygen, some OTC drugs such as ephedrine (based on the amount found), and other substances. Finally, some toxicologists work with animals such as racehorses, looking for performance-enhancing substances.

Although testing for alcohol and performance-enhancing substances is becoming more familiar, the public most often associates forensic toxicology with its other major division, postmortem toxicology. Samples for this type of work are obtained during autopsy and consist of bodily fluids, organs, and bones. The table indicates typical

Urine is used frequently in drug testing for sports and in the workplace. This image shows urine samples for doping analysis at a doping institute in Kreischa, Germany, October 30, 2003. *(Ralf Hirschberger/DPA/Landov)*

materials, those that are routinely collected. Other samples may be taken depending on what type of drugs or poisons might be present. In cases where a body is not found until long after death there may be no blood or flesh left. In these situations more durable materials such as bone may be all that is available. If a victim is trapped in a fire and dies, similar problems will arise due to the burn damage inflicted on the body.

A relatively new branch of postmortem toxicology is entomotoxicology, referring to entomology, the study of insects. Suppose a person who has taken a large dose of a drug such as cocaine wanders into the woods and dies in a place where the body is not found for weeks. Decomposition will mean that there is no blood or tissue that could be

Sports Toxicology

Obtaining samples from athletes shares many similarities with forensic sampling. The samples must be collected under tightly controlled conditions in which there is no question from whom or where the sample came. The samples must be kept safe and covered by a chain-of-custody document indicating who had control of the samples from collection through analysis and disposal. How these requirements are met is governed by the sports authority that oversees that particular sport and athlete.

The National Collegiate Athletic Association, for example, stipulates how urine is to be collected for analysis for what it classifies as banned

Lab technician Li Zhang performs a density test from urine samples at the Australian Sports Drug Testing Laboratory in Sydney, September 1, 2000. Starting the following day, the Australian Sports Drug Agency was contracted by the International Olympic Committee to conduct at least 400 pre–Olympic Games tests. *(AP Photo/Rick Rycroft)*

used for samples. Within minutes of death insects arrive on the body, which becomes the basis of a small ecosystem. The first insects to arrive are flies, followed by successive waves of other insects that feed on the body and/or on other insects already there. The insects that feed on the body consume the cocaine that the person had taken as well. In some cases it is possible to analyze the insects and discover cocaine or cocaine metabolites within their bodies. The same is true of many drugs and poisons; their presence in insects can indicate that the deceased person had taken them just prior to death.

The third general area of toxicology that has forensic aspects is the type used in workplace drug testing. People who work in law enforcement, many government agencies, and many private companies are

substances. Interestingly, not all of the banned substances are illegal drugs. They are prohibited, however, because an athlete taking them may have an unfair advantage over other athletes who do not take them. The procedure for collection starts when the athlete arrives at a collection station, where he or she selects a beaker to use. Until the athlete delivers 85 ml of urine (while being watched by a crew chief), he or she stays in the collection station. If the athlete is unable to deliver enough urine in one event, he or she can drink approved beverages from sealed containers kept at the collection station for such situations.

The urine must have a pH between 4.5 and 7.5 and a specific gravity of above 1.005 (any lower suggests the possibility of dilution). Once the urine meets these specifications, it is divided into two containers, approximately 60 ml in "A" and the rest in "B." Both the crew chief and athlete witness all these steps, including the creation of the chain-of-custody forms. The samples are then delivered to the laboratory for testing. The results are used to insure that the athlete is not using banned substances.

POSTMORTEM SAMPLES USED IN TOXICOLOGY

	Specimen	Amount
always collected	blood (heart)	25 ml
always collected	blood (drawn peripherally)	10 ml
always collected	urine	all
usually collected	vitreous humor (fluid behind the lens of the eye)	all
usually collected	gastric contents	all
usually collected	bile	all
usually collected	brain	100 g
usually collected	liver	100 g
usually collected	kidney	50 g
usually collected	hair	varies
collected in some cases	spleen	varies
collected in some cases	fatty tissue (adipose)	varies
collected in some cases	lung	varies
collected in some cases	muscle tissue	varies
collected in some cases	insects (forensic entomology)	varies
collected in some cases	bone marrow	varies
collected in some cases	intestine	varies

required to undergo drug testing as a condition of their hiring or maintaining a job. The substance tested is urine, and the procedures for collection are strict and tightly controlled. This type of toxicology is performed in private toxicology laboratories, and the practice of workplace drug testing is becoming quite common both in government and private settings.

POISONS

Broadly speaking, there are three classes of poisons studied by forensic toxicologists. The first are those of plant origin, such as hemlock and strychnine. The second type is the heavy metals (and other elements), including arsenic, thallium, lead, mercury, beryllium, and cadmium. The third class contains gases, including carbon monoxide (CO) and hydrogen cyanide (HCN), which was once used in gas chamber executions. Powdered cyanide, most often in the form of sodium cyanide (NaCN) or potassium cyanide (KCN), is a lethal poison in its own right that falls outside these loose divisions.

KCN was used in the Tylenol tampering case in 1982 that occurred in Chicago. In that case powdered cyanide was added to several bottles of Tylenol, resulting in the death of seven people and the classification of product tampering as a federal offense. Forensic chemists working that

The Death of Socrates by Charles Alphonse Dufresnoy (1611–68). Created in 1650, the painting is in the Galleria Palatina of the Palazzo Pitti, Florence, Italy. *(Alinari/Art Resource)*

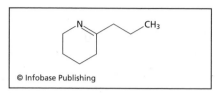

The structure of coniine, the toxin in hemlock

© Infobase Publishing

year were inundated with suspicious powders submitted by a nervous public and law-enforcement officials. A similar situation occurred in 2001 in the immediate aftermath of the anthrax mailings. In that incident a still unknown person or persons sent anthrax powder through the mail to several places along the East Coast of the United States. More than 20 people developed an infection, and five died.

Plant poisons generally belong to a chemical class called alkaloids, the same group that contains caffeine. According to an account written by the Greek philosopher Plato, Socrates was executed by being forced to drink an extract of a plant that is presumed to have been hemlock. The hemlock plant, *Conium maculatum,* was known to be poisonous, acting on the nervous system and causing paralysis. The toxic agent in hemlock is called coniine. Other plant poisons include atropine (extracted from the nightshade plant, *Atropa belladonna*) and many species of mushrooms. Since September 11, 2001, there has been increasing concern about a poison called ricin, which can be extracted from castor beans (*Ricin communis*). The toxin is a complex protein molecule that in small doses can stop critical cell functions and cause death. In late 2003 and 2004 the FBI reported that several offices in Washington, D.C., had received letters that contained a powdery material suspected to contain ricin. The poison is much more lethal when injected than inhaled or ingested.

Once forensic toxicology was an established science and laboratory methods became reliable, the use of metals as poisons dropped dramatically. Heavy-metal poisoning still occurs but mostly by accidental exposure from materials in the environment. Lead, once a common ingredient in paint, still poisons children who eat or otherwise ingest paint chips that contain it. Lead is also found as an environmental contaminant of soils and waters. As with many heavy metal poisons, its effects tend to be more severe in children than in adults. Mercury is another environmental poison, particularly when it is in the form of methyl mercury or dimethyl mercury (CH_3-Hg-CH_3).

Of the three major categories of poisons toxic gases are responsible for a large number of deaths each year. One culprit is CO, produced as a by-product of combustion. Anytime there is a fire or open flame, significant amounts of CO can be produced. Cars are based on internal combustion, so car exhaust contains CO. As a result vehicle exhaust is sufficiently poisonous to kill and is not an uncommon method of committing suicide. Accidental CO poisoning occurs when heaters that use flames malfunction or are brought into a home. Barbeque grills and propane stoves can produce significant amounts of CO, and every year several deaths result from faulty heaters during the winter months, when homes are typically sealed up tight.

Another combustion product, HCN, is a very toxic substance that can also be formed when synthetic materials such as plastics or fabrics burn. Normally a person who does not smoke will have a trace level of cyanide in his or her blood. Smokers have about twice that level, or around 0.04 µg/ml. Amounts that exceed about 2.5 µg/ml can be quickly fatal. Another way HCN is produced is when an acid is added to a powdered form of cyanide, which is how HCN was generated in gas chamber executions.

Measurement of CO and cyanide levels in blood is especially useful when a person is found dead after a fire. The immediate forensic question is "Did this person die as a result of the fire or was he or she dead before?" If the person was breathing during the fire, there will be elevated levels of both compounds in the person's blood. If the person was not breathing when the fire was burning, the levels should be near normal. The longer the victim was breathing during the fire, the higher the levels. This testing is important because in murder cases it is not unusual for the killer(s) to attempt to destroy evidence by setting a fire. In these cases the findings of the forensic toxicologist are critical.

Given the progress in forensic chemistry and forensic toxicology, intentional poisoning as a means to commit murder is rare. This does not mean that there is no poisoning, just that the use of poison as a murder weapon has greatly decreased as the skill and expertise of forensic chemists and forensic toxicologists have increased. Nor does this mean the end of poisoning, just that most poisonings now are accidental or the result of environmental exposure. In 2005 more than 2 million cases of poisoning were reported to the American Association of Poison Control

Centers. Of these more than 1,200 cases resulted in death. Of the total number of reported incidents nearly 84 percent were accidental or unintentional poisonings. Sadly, a large number of poisonings are also self-inflicted as a means of committing suicide, with just over 8 percent of the reported poisonings attributed to suicides or suicide attempts. Malicious poisonings accounted for less than 1 percent of the total reported poisonings, a low number that has much to do with progress in forensic chemistry and the skill of forensic toxicologists.

4

Forensic Drug Analysis

The main difference between forensic toxicology and forensic drug analysis is the sample types. Toxicologists work with drugs and poisons found in the blood, bodily fluids, and tissues, while forensic chemists work with the drugs and poisons before they are ingested. In a typical local or state crime laboratory drug cases represent the largest caseload and work that the laboratory performs. Of those cases the largest single group of cases usually involves marijuana.

The job of the forensic drug analyst is to identify any illegal substances found in exhibits or to prove conclusively that no illegal drugs or substances are present. This is accomplished by successive classification followed by definitive identification. But to understand this process it is helpful to answer two fundamental questions: First, what is a drug? Secondly, how exactly does a chemist classify a drug?

WHAT IS A DRUG?

It has already been shown that everything can be a poison, but the same is not true of a drug. A drug can be a poison, but not all poisons are drugs. A drug is a substance that when ingested is capable of inducing a change in the body's chemistry. Drugs are used to treat or prevent disease, to reduce pain, to promote sleep, and so on. Medicines are combinations of drugs and inert ingredients. For example, an aspirin tablet that contains nothing but aspirin is a drug, while a tablet taken to treat the symptoms of a cold is a medicine, because it contains separate ingredients for a runny nose, congestion, coughing, aches, sore throat, and a fever. The terms *drug* and *medicine* are often used interchangeably, despite this distinction.

Obviously not all drugs or medicines are illegal. There are two factors that are important when a government agency decides if possessing a drug is illegal. First, if the drug has a potential to be abused, then it is likely to be controlled in some way, as abuse could cause harm. Second, if a drug has a legitimate medical use, then it must still be available to doctors and pharmacists to provide to patients who need it. The government must weigh the legitimate needs and uses of a drug against its ability to be abused and to cause harm when deciding how to regulate it.

The definition of drug abuse changes over time and differs among societies. Cocaine was once an ingredient in Coca-Cola, LSD was used in psychotherapy and by the CIA, and methamphetamine was issued to American soldiers during World War II. All three drugs are regarded as dangerous today, and they are no longer used in these ways. Meanwhile, the active ingredient in marijuana has been found to be useful in treating glaucoma, anorexia, and the nausea associated with chemotherapy. A drug, Marinol (dronabinol), now exists that contains the active ingredients of marijuana. The list of illegal or controlled drugs is therefore flexible and evolves. What tends to remain the same is the methods used to group and classify drugs.

SYSTEMS OF DRUG CLASSIFICATION

Chemists usually describe drugs based on their chemical properties. Some drugs, such as aspirin, are acidic. If an aspirin tablet is dissolved in water, the pH of the water will become slightly acidic, comparable to vinegar or diluted lemon juice. The active ingredients in marijuana are also slightly acidic. Most drugs are weak bases and as a result have a bitter taste. Caffeine, found in coffee, tea, and many sodas, is a basic

What a Difference a Century Makes

"Cocaine will make the coward brave, the silent eloquent and free victims of alcohol and opium from their bondage."
—Park Davis, pharmaceutical advertisement*

The original formula for Coca-Cola was invented by chemist John S. Pemberton, whose goal was to create the perfect medicinal drink. He had heard about extracts of the coca plant and knew of the purported stimulant and aphrodisiac effects. His first concoction was Pemberton's French Wine Cola, launched in 1885. It sold particularly well in Atlanta, Georgia. He continued striving to make a "temperance drink" based on coca extracts and the kola nut but without the bitter taste typical of alkaloids such as cocaine and caffeine. Pemberton found that the addition of sugar and corn syrup helped, along with some citric acid to counter any oversweetening. The name Coca-Cola came from the drink's two key ingredients. Pemberton sold the company when he became ill with cancer, but work continued on the formula, although public sentiment was turning

Dr. John S. Pemberton, who invented Coca-Cola (© Topham/ The Image Works)

against cocaine given the potential for addiction by the turn of the century. Cocaine was out of the formula by 1929.

* Quoted in "Drug Enforcement Administration: Historical Interviews, James McGivency, Tape no. 162." Available online. URL: http://www. deamuseum.org/transcripts/jamesmcgiveney_11042003.pdf. Downloaded January 2, 2008.

Coca-Cola ad, 1914, from an American magazine *(The Granger Collection)*

(alkaline) drug that has a distinctive bitter taste. Illegal drugs such as cocaine, heroin, and methamphetamine are also basic.

One group of basic drugs, the alkaloids, is particularly important. The alkaloids are, or were at one time, obtained from seed plants. An older term for these substances is *vegetable base*. Caffeine is an alkaloid, as are cocaine and heroin. Within the alkaloid family caffeine is a xan-thine alkaloid, a class that also includes theophylline, an ingredient in tea and chocolate. Cocaine is a tropane alkaloid, a class characterized by a bridge in their molecular structure. Heroin is an opiate alkaloid, a class of drugs that are found in or made from the opium poppy.

Another way forensic chemists classify drugs is by how they are obtained. Drugs that come directly from plants are referred to as natural drugs or natural products. Marijuana and cocaine are natural products because they can be extracted directly from plants. If a drug is made by a chemical reaction with a plant extract, that drug is called semi-synthetic. Heroin is a semi-synthetic because it is made by a reaction of a chemical (acetic anhydride) with the compound morphine, which is contained in the opium extract. The morphine is, like cocaine, a natural product, but it takes additional chemical treatment to convert it to heroin. Synthetic drugs are made from scratch in the laboratory. Methamphetamine and many prescription drugs are synthetic. Finally, hormones and steroids are considered drugs and are obtained or synthesized from animals, humans, or genetically engineered bacteria. An example is the drug insulin, used to control diabetes.

This classification of natural, semi-synthetic, and synthetic is becom-ing more difficult to use as techniques and capabilities of synthetic chemists advance. Compounds that were once obtained only from plant matter, such as tetrahydrocannabinol (THC), the active ingredient in marijuana, can now be synthesized and is used in the drug Marinol mentioned previously. However, there are several other classification methods that are still useful.

Forensic chemists, physicians, and other health care professionals often categorize drugs based on the type of effect they have when taken, as in the following categories.

- *Analgesics*: These are drugs that relieve pain, such as aspirin, ibuprofen, naproxen sodium, and morphine. Aspirin and related drugs are called nonsteroidal anti-inflammatory drugs (NSAIDs), a group of drugs that stop pain by reducing fever and inflammation. Morphine and other opiates reduce pain by attaching to specific sites scattered throughout the central nervous system (CNS). By doing so they block transmission of nerve impulses that relay the sensation of pain to the brain. Aspirin reduces pain by inhibiting the processes that cause it, while morphine intercepts the pain signal after it is produced. The side effects of morphine lead it to be classified also as a narcotic. The different mechanisms explain why morphine is addictive and aspirin is not and also why morphine has a high potential for abuse and aspirin a low potential.

- *Depressants*: These drugs depress functions of the CNS resulting in slowed heartbeat, reduction of anxiety, and, in some cases, promotion of sleep. Barbiturates, tranquilizers, alcohol (ethanol), and sleep aids are depressants.

- *Hallucinogens*: These are drugs that alter the perception of time and reality. Movement, thought, perceptions, vision, and hearing are also affected. LSD, mescaline, and marijuana are examples.

- *Narcotics*: These are drugs that have analgesic effects, depress the CNS, and tend to promote sleep. Opiate alkaloids (drugs derived from the opium plant) are the best known narcotics, and this group includes morphine, codeine, heroin, hydromorphone, oxycodone, and methadone.

- *Stimulants*: These are drugs that stimulate functions of the CNS, induce alertness, and prevent sleep. Cocaine, amphetamine, and methamphetamine are stimulants. At high doses many stimulants are hallucinogenic.

Classification by general effect is useful not only to forensic chemists but also to health care professionals and the general public.

Another system used in forensic chemistry groups drugs based on how they are used and abused. Their structures are often similar, as are the physiological effects. Most of these substances will be discussed individually later. Four such classes are the following:

- *Predator drugs*: Also known as date rape drugs, these are substances that are used to incapacitate a person (typically a woman) for sexual purposes. Current date rape drugs, aside from alcohol, are ketamine, Rohypnol, and gamma hydroxybutyrate (GHB) and related compounds. When a predator drug is mixed in a drink, the effects can range from disorientation to unconsciousness and loss of short-term memory.

- *Club drugs*: Drugs used recreationally at parties and clubs frequented by young people get this designation; many of these drugs are also predator drugs. Examples include ketamine, Rohypnol, and Ecstasy (MDMA), a stimulant and mild hallucinogen related to amphetamine. Other hallucinogens such as LSD and psilocybin mushrooms are sometimes included in this group, as are PCP (phencyclidine) and methamphetamine. One apparent reason for their popularity is the misconception that the club drugs are less dangerous than drugs such as cocaine and heroin.

- *Human performance drugs*: This group includes substances that improve or impair performance, most notably anabolic steroids and alcohol. The former consists of dozens of drugs, mostly prescription drugs, based on the male hormone testosterone. These are abused by athletes as young as high school age in attempts to increase their muscle mass and decrease recovery time after strenuous training and competition.

- *Inhalants*: Substances that are inhaled, most of which are not drugs at all, include paint thinners, nitrous oxide, gasoline, cleaners, nail polishes, and so on. Essentially any substance that has a volatile component can be used as an inhalant, and in general these substances have depressant effects similar to those of alcohol.

The above terms are convenient for grouping types of drugs according to their illicit uses. These descriptions are also fluid because a drug can sometimes belong to more than one category of abuse. Rohypnol, for example, finds illicit use as both a date rape drug and a club drug. The basis for the final system of classifying a drug is more rigid: its legal status in the United States.

CLASSIFICATION BY SCHEDULE: THE CONTROLLED SUBSTANCES ACT AND LISTED CHEMICALS

For the forensic chemist the legal categorization of a drug is nearly as important as the chemical and physiological one. If a drug is described as a "drug of abuse," this generally means that the drug or compounds related to it that have fallen subject to regulations and laws. In turn, this typically occurs because the drug or related compounds have potential to be abused and to cause harm.

Abused drugs tend to be those that produce significant psychological and physiological effects. The example of morphine is typical; it suppresses pain and in the process can produce a feeling of well-being or euphoria. In contrast, aspirin stops pain but is not associated with mood-altering side effects and so has a low potential for abuse. Abused drugs are usually addictive physiologically, psychologically, or both. Morphine falls into this category as well. Users take the drug initially for the pleasant psychological effects but can quickly become addicted. Users often develop tolerances for the abused drug, meaning that ever-increasing doses are needed to elicit the desired effect.

In the United States drugs are regulated under the Controlled Substances Act (CSA), passed in 1970. The CSA divides drugs into "schedules" based on their medical uses and potential for abuse as shown in the table. The act specifies penalties for violations, ranging up to 20 years in prison and $1 million in fines for the first offense involving Schedule I substances down to a maximum of one year in prison and $100,000 in fines for a first offense involving a Schedule V substance.

The CSA took aim primarily at drugs, and lawmakers addressed the materials used to synthesize many of them. Drugs such as PCP, GHB, and methamphetamine are relatively simple to make, requiring basic chemistry skills. An effective tool to minimize illicit production is to limit access to the drug's precursors (chemical ingredients). Accordingly, the CSA has been modified over the years to include many of the key precursor chemicals needed for making methamphetamine and other clandestinely prepared drugs such as PCP. Rather than listing all its precursors as controlled substances, Congress passed the Chemical Diversion and Trafficking Act (CDTA) in 1988 and amended it in 1993. This created two lists of chemicals that are regulated principally to deter their diversion for clandestine drug synthesis.

CONTROLLED SUBSTANCES AND THE CONTROLLED SUBSTANCES ACT

Schedule	Medical use	Controls on prescriptions	Required security	Potential for abuse	Addiction potential	Examples
I	none accepted	not available by prescription; used only for research	vault or safe	highest	severe	LSD, heroin, MDMA (Ecstasy), marijuana, GHB
II	some accepted uses with restrictions	written prescription with no refills	vault or safe		severe	morphine and many related opiates, cocaine, amphetamine and methamphetamine, most barbiturates, oxycodone
III	accepted uses	written or oral (phone-in), limits on refills and time	secured area		moderate to low	ketamine, anabolic steroids, some codeine preparations
IV	accepted uses	written or oral (phone-in), limits on refills and time	secured area		limited	benzodiazepines such as valium, mild sleep aids
V	accepted uses	over the counter or written or oral (phone-in), limits on refills and time	secured area	lowest	limited	selected preparations of codeine

Source: U.S. Drug Enforcement Administration. URL: http://www.usdoj.gov/dea/index. Access Web site for most current version.

It is important to realize that drugs can be classified in different systems. Rohypnol, for example, is an abused drug of concern to forensic chemists. It is classified as a basic drug, a benzodiazepine, synthetic, a hypnotic/sedative, a predator drug, and a Schedule IV drug. Forensic chemists must be aware of all of these classifications as part of their analysis of drug evidence.

DRUGS AS EVIDENCE

The analysis of materials suspected to be or to contain controlled substances represents the largest portion of the workload in most forensic laboratories. When suspected controlled substances are submitted as physical evidence (exhibits), the forensic chemist must identify and in some cases quantify the controlled substances present. The most common forms of evidence seen can be summarized as the "five p's:" powders, plant matter, pills, precursors, and paraphernalia.

Powders run the gamut of crystalline white to resinous brown. Hashish, a concentrated form of marijuana, lies between plant and powder. Many powders are oily and odiferous, while others can only be described (unofficially and informally) as goo. Typical plant matter exhibits are marijuana, mushrooms, and cactus buttons. As biological evidence, plant matter must be stored properly to prevent rotting and degradation prior to analysis; failure to do so can create goo.

Pills such as prescription medications or clandestinely synthesized tablets are common forms of physical evidence. In cases where the evidence is or appears to be commercially manufactured drugs (OTC or prescription), tentative identifications can be made visually using references such as the *Physician's Desk Reference*. In other cases the pills may have other markings such as crosses or imprints. Amphetamines, methamphetamine, and LSD are often sold illicitly in pill form, although typically the pills are cruder than those produced commercially.

Precursors are compounds or materials used in the clandestine synthesis of drugs such as methamphetamine. Immediate precursors are those that require only one or two simple steps to convert the controlled substance, while distant precursors require more steps. Some precursors are controlled and listed on schedules of the CSA, while others are not. For example, 1-phenylcyclohexylamine (PC) and 1-piperidinocyclohexanecarbonitrile (PCC) are listed on Schedule II; both are precursors used to synthesize phencyclidine (PCP), a Schedule II substance. Likewise, phenyl acetone (phenyl-2-propanone, or P2P) was once the preferred starting point for illicit methamphetamine; it is now listed on Schedule II. Lysergic acid and lysergic acid amide, precursors of LSD, are listed on Schedule III. Other precursors are not necessarily controlled but must still be identified as part of investigations of clandestine synthesis.

Drug paraphernalia are the implements and equipment used to prepare and ingest drugs. Typical items include syringes (a significant biohazard to the analyst), cookers used to prepare heroin and other drugs, pipes and bongs (water-filled vessels) used in smoking marijuana, and razor blades, mirrors, and straws used for snorting cocaine. Such items present a sampling and analytical challenge since only traces of material may remain. Typically analysts rinse the items with a solvent to extract the residues, a destructive step that significantly alters an entire evidence exhibit.

Of the five p's the most frequently submitted by numbers of cases is plant matter suspected of being or containing marijuana. Methamphetamine, cocaine, amphetamine, and heroin are also common, although the order and numbers vary across regions and states. The last 10 years have seen increasing incidence of use of predator drugs, methamphetamine, and MDMA, while rates of cocaine and heroin appear to have stabilized. Different states and regions deal with different problems: Hawaii and West Virginia are hotspots of marijuana production; Washington State grapples with more than 1,000 clandestine laboratories; and border states, north and south, struggle to stem the flow of smuggled drugs.

Forensic chemistry being what it is, forensic chemists may unexpectedly encounter other types of evidence. For instance, although one of its street names is angel dust, phencyclidine is a controlled substance often seized in liquid form, usually a greenish solution with an overwhelming smell. Spray cans, bags, or rags soaked with inhalants can turn up in forensic laboratories. The day after Halloween can bring an interesting array of submissions, such as suspect apples and candy bars.

DILUENTS AND ADULTERANTS

In addition to identifying and quantifying illicit drugs themselves, forensic chemists often must identify cutting agents added to many drug exhibits. Clandestine chemists use cutting agents to stretch the supply of a controlled substance and maximize profits. Cutting agents are often chosen based on their chemical similarity to the controlled substance being produced. Heroin has a bitter taste mimicked by quinine. Cocaine is an anesthetic used to numb the eye for eye surgery, so it should be no surprise that cocaine is often cut with a local anesthetic such as Novocain. Other common cutting agents include sugars such as mannitol and inositol and less frequently baking soda, caffeine, and table sugar. Starches such as cornstarch are also common. Identification of diluents is an important part of drug profiling, discussed in the next section.

Just like drugs, cutting agents are categorized. Diluents (thinners) are substances that are not drugs. Baking soda and sugars fall into this category. Adulterants are pharmacologically active and typically have effects that are grossly similar to the drug. Caffeine added to cocaine is an example where both the drug and the adulterant are stimulants.

Aside from cutting agents, impurities are materials that occur naturally with the drug (if a natural product) or are added to it inadvertently during processing. Consider a cup of tea, which is a natural product obtained from plant matter. It is not a pure substance, but contains many different alkaloids including caffeine and theophylline. The same is true of illicit drugs obtained directly or indirectly from plant matter such as cocaine or heroin. Finally, contaminants are substances that find their way into the sample by accident. If heroin is extracted using lime $(Ca(OH)_2)$ and the lime is contaminated with sand, the sand that ends up in the heroin is a contaminant that originated as a contaminant in the lime.

The cutting agents and other materials that are found in illicit drugs—diluents, adulterants, impurities, and contaminants—are all of interest to the forensic chemist as he or she conducts the process of drug profiling.

PROFILING

Profiling a drug sample means analyzing the composition beyond simple identification and quantitation of the controlled substance(s) present. It is a more detailed analysis that leads to what is sometimes called a "chemical fingerprint." The goal of profiling is to identify what processing or synthetic methods were used to make a drug. If the drug is a natural product such as cocaine or heroin, another goal is to identify the geographic region where the plant was grown. Often the information obtained through profiling is used to categorize drug samples into similar groups to provide investigative information such as common origin. The road from the fields or the clandestine lab to the street and to the forensic lab has many steps, each of which can add distinctiveness to the sample batch.

The first step in profiling starts with a description of color, appearance (sparkling powder versus oily, for example), and microscopic characterization of diluents, such as starches or sugars. The examination then becomes more complex and interesting as the analyst may test for isotope ratios, co-extracted components, impurities, adulterants and diluents, and even the DNA of plants that are part of the process.

Measurements of stable isotope ratios (SIRs) have long been used in ecological and botanical research. Isotopes of an element have the same number of protons in the nucleus of their atoms but a different number of neutrons. Most elements have stable, naturally occurring isotopes. For example, the most abundant form of carbon has six protons and six neutrons in the nucleus and is called carbon 12 or ^{12}C. However, of all the carbon atoms on Earth, about 1 percent have an extra neutron in the nucleus, known as ^{13}C. The common form of oxygen is ^{16}O, but ^{18}O also exists. These are examples of what are called "stable isotopes" because they are found in relatively stable ratios. ^{13}C abundance is usually 1 percent of that of ^{12}C, for example. When the ratios differ from the normal proportion, this provides important information. Any process that alters the normal ratio of stable isotopes is called fractionation, and forensic chemists can use data like this in profiling.

Isotopes of an element are chemically identical. This means that ^{12}C and ^{13}C behave chemically the same way. The only difference between them is their mass since ^{13}C has an extra neutron. The same is true of isotopes of oxygen, nitrogen, and so on. Since isotopes are chemically identical, fractionation is caused by the mass differences. For example, ^{18}O constitutes approximately 0.2 percent of all oxygen found on Earth. A water molecule that incorporates ^{18}O is slightly heavier than a molecule containing the more common ^{16}O isotope. The "heavier" water will need slightly more energy to evaporate from the liquid phase into the gas phase. Similarly, when rain or snow falls, gravity favors heavier isotopes over lighter ones and more of the lighter compounds will evaporate compared to the heavier ones. These are examples of abiotic (nonbiological) fractionation processes. Biological processes also lead to fractionation, although the basis of this fractionation is purely physical and not chemical. For example, when water evaporates from a leaf surface, water molecules incorporating lighter isotopes evaporate more quickly than molecules containing heavier isotopes. As a result the leaf becomes enriched in the heavier isotopes. Similar cycles and interactions can be identified for nitrogen, a key nutrient for plants.

Why are these processes and ratios important to a forensic chemist? If the drug involved in an investigation comes from a plant, the isotope ratios can tell the story of when, where, and how the plant grew. The isotopic ratios within a plant are the result of numerous and complex fractionation processes that are unique to a region and that depend on climate, temperature, precipitation, elevation, season, and soil. Plants from the same place will have similar isotope ratios, while those grown in different soils or even in the same soil at a different time will have different ratios. For plant-derived drugs isotopic ratio analysis can provide information on geographical region of origin, but only if trustworthy standards are available for comparison. Just like human fingerprints, one chemical fingerprint is only useful if there is a standard comparison.

Co-extracted components are another set of characteristics that forensic chemists analyze as part of profiling. With drugs derived from plants there are always alkaloids extracted along with the drug or its precursor. In the case of opium, morphine is the target compound and precursor to heroin, but other alkaloids are inevitably carried throughout processing. Codeine, thebaine, papaverine, noscapine, and other trace alkaloids will be extracted along with the morphine and will interact and react along with morphine as processing continues. These ratios of opium alkaloids and chemical derivatives are similar within a batch but variable outside that batch. Additionally, because of their chemical similarity, analytical methods such as TLC, GC-MS, or HPLC (described previously) optimized for heroin or cocaine usually will also separate and identify these impurities. As a result analysis of impurities can be performed simultaneously with the necessary evidentiary analysis.

Each stage of processing introduces impurities to a batch, much as any laboratory analysis can be contaminated by impure reagents or dirty glassware. Acids and bases can be contaminated with trace metals and ions, as can water. Solvents can carry organic contaminants or be contaminants themselves. Residual solvents and any characteristic impurities contained can be trapped within the powdered drug. Use of different solvents at different stages adds further to residuals. Because residual solvents are likely to be found in higher concentrations that trace contaminants of reagents, they have become part of profiling methodologies.

Adulterants and diluents added to a batch of an illicit drug can provide useful information regarding batches and groups. Adulterants common in heroin are acetaminophen (the active ingredient in Tylenol), caffeine, and lidocaine, all of which chromatograph well and can be detected simultaneously with the heroin. Diluents tend to be more variable, running the gamut from baking soda to sugars and quinine. Many of these are harder to identify as part of routine analysis since some are removed during sample preparation steps. Even if diluents can be isolated, identification often requires more time than can be spared in routine cases. Sometimes a quick microscopic examination of residues is sufficient to identify starches or sugars, but often more specialized testing is needed.

Finally, when the drug is a plant, there is another option for profiling. As a plant, marijuana has DNA, which allows for typing and grouping of samples as well as definitive identification of the species, something that chemical tests cannot achieve. This work is in the early stages and may become in a few years, an important profiling tool available to forensic chemists. While profiling of drugs is not routinely done in most cases, it can provide investigators with invaluable investigative information. However, the primary job of most forensic drug chemists is to identify what drug or drugs are present in physical evidence.

EXAMPLES OF ILLEGAL DRUGS

The types of drugs analyzed by forensic chemists vary depending on location and many other factors. In the United States the most abused illegal drug is marijuana. Other commonly abused drugs include cocaine, heroin, and methamphetamine. The prescription drug Oxycontin (containing oxycodone) is becoming a significant problem as are drugs that fall into the date rape and club drug categories. As laws and society change, so do drug abuse patterns.

Marijuana is a plant that has been used as a medicine since ancient times. The tough, weedy plant is grown for fiber as well as for illegal use. The fiber is called hemp and can be made into clothing or rope. The term *marijuana* refers to drugs derived from the plant *Cannabis sativa* and specifically to the leaves and flowering tops of those plants. The active chemical ingredients collectively are referred to as the tetrahydrocannabinols, which are classified as hallucinogens. Users ingest these oily compounds by smoking the leaves of the marijuana plant.

Marijuana is the most widely abused illegal substance in the United States, with recent data showing that nearly half of all high school seniors had tried it at least once. It is classified as a hallucinogen and is listed on Schedule I. The marijuana plant can grow to more than five feet in height. The cannabinol of most concern in marijuana and its derivatives is delta-9-tetrahydrocannabinol, usually abbreviated simply as THC. Through careful cultivation, the THC content of the plant has steadily increased and now is in the range of 3 to 5 percent for leaves and flowers. Hashish, or hash oil, is the oily resin excreted by the flowering tops and has a higher concentration of THC, in the range of 10 to 20 percent. Sinsemilla, a variety of marijuana plant developed in the late 1970s, has THC content in the range of 10 percent. Within any marijuana plant the THC content is highest in the resins and lowest in seeds.

It is thought that Napoleon's soldiers first brought marijuana to Europe when they returned from the Middle East, and that it made its way into the United States around 1910 by way of Mexican immigrant labor. The drug is almost always taken by smoking, although recently oral preparations have become available for the treatment of discomfort and nausea associated with chemotherapy. Since the drug is smoked in the form of cigarettes (joints), the process carries the same hazards as any smoking including increased risk of cancer proportionate to the degree of use. Marijuana is somewhat unusual in that the effects (depressant, stimulant, and/or hallucinogenic effects, along with increases in appetite) produced is proportionate to amount ingested.

Forensic analysis of marijuana begins with an evaluation of botanical structures of the plant, including microscopic features called cystolithic hairs. Informally, these are called bear claws because of their distinctive shape. The presence of these structures is strong evidence of the presence of marijuana but not definitive evidence. The modified Duquenois-Levine test is a presumptive test for THC, which can be performed on the plant matter, resins, or seeds. The confirmatory test for the identification is often TLC. In forensic toxicology the challenge is to detect THC and its metabolites in tissues and body fluids, primarily urine. This can be accomplished by immunoassay, which is coupled to confirmatory techniques. Similar techniques can be used to detect THC in saliva.

Another well-known plant-derived drug is cocaine. Cocaine is a powerful central nervous system stimulant derived from the leaves of the coca plant (*Erythroxylon coca*). Cocaine can also be synthesized, but the process is difficult and expensive and so far has not replaced the coca plant as the primary source in the illegal drug market. The coca plant grows in the Andes Mountains and in some parts of Asia, and the largest source of raw coca is South America, principally Colombia. Natives of the region chewed on the leaves and brewed teas that they used medicinally (they still do), and Sigmund Freud, who used it and wrote glowingly about the drug in the 1880s, popularized cocaine in the modern era. Extracts of the coca leaf were also ingredients in Coca-Cola and other medicinal preparations in the early 20th century.

Cocaine has legitimate medical uses as a topical anesthetic in the eyes, nose, and throat, producing the same numbing effect as Novocain (procaine). However, other related compounds have largely replaced cocaine in these roles. Illicit cocaine is supplied as the hydrochloride salt, a crystalline white powder, usually diluted with cutting agents such as lidocaine, sugars, or caffeine. The hydrochloride salt can be converted to the free base form by dissolving the salt in water and heating gently with baking soda or ammonia. The base form is typically smoked, producing an immediate response that is almost as fast as that obtained by injection. The effects of cocaine on the user are similar to that of amphetamine and methamphetamine: elevated heart rate, rapid breathing, and a feeling of alertness and well-being. The primary source of cocaine for the U.S. market is Colombia, and the drug is often smuggled through

Arizona, Florida, California, and Texas. Cocaine usage has declined from its peak in the 1980s, but data from the National Household Survey on Drug Abuse still showed that in 2006 approximately 1 percent of the U.S. population, or about 2.4 million people, had used cocaine in the past month. The analysis of cocaine involves the use of presumptive tests such as cobalt thiocyanate, crystal tests (gold chloride and platinum chloride), TLC, and GC-MS. IR spectroscopy is also used.

Heroin is a derivative of morphine that is highly addictive and widely abused. Also called diacetylmorphine, diamorphine, and acetomorphine, heroin is easily synthesized from morphine by the addition of acetyl chloride or acetic anhydride. The morphine in turn is obtained from opium poppies, and so heroin is classified as one of the opiate alkaloids. It is most commonly found in the form of a hydrochloride salt with a white or off-white color; however, a brownish black resinous form known as black tar is also seen. Heroin is water soluble and users typically ingest heroin by injection, although snorting and smoking are possible. Because of its potency, heroin is both physically and psychologically addictive and has no acceptable medical use. It is listed on Schedule I of the CSA.

Heroin is often mixed with various cutting agents such as quinine. Sugars, powdered milk, procaine, lidocaine, and in the case of darker-colored heroin cocoa may also be used. Heroin use increased during the 1990s, but there are signs that it has since leveled off. Sources of heroin are Mexico, South America, Asia, and southwest Asia (Turkey, Afghanistan, and the neighboring regions). The analytical approach to heroin is similar to that used for cocaine and involves combinations of presumptive tests, crystal tests (gold chloride and platinum chloride), TLC, and GC-MS. IR spectroscopy is also used.

The amphetamine family includes the stimulants amphetamine, dextroamphetamine, and methamphetamine, which were once freely prescribed for weight control, fatigue, and narcolepsy (a sleeping disorder also known as sleeping sickness). Both amphetamine and methamphetamine were used during World War II as a stimulant for troops, and after the war they were used by truckers, dieters, and athletes. As abuse spread, the federal government limited the amount of amphetamines that could be manufactured and removed many types from the market. As a result illegal demand for the drug is now supplied primarily by clandestine laboratories. Street names for the drugs include speed, ice, crystal, and Bennies, depending on identity and form. Data provided by the 2006 National Household Survey on Drug Abuse indicated that there were 731,000 current users of methamphetamine aged 12 or older.

Amphetamines stimulate the sympathetic nervous system, which controls heart rate, blood pressure, and respiration, and excessive use can lead to severe effects such as hallucinations, convulsions, prickling of the skin, unpredictable emotional swings, extreme aggression, and death. They can be taken orally, snorted, injected, or smoked. Amphetamines are psychologically addictive, but debate continues as to the degree of physiological dependence they produce. A dangerous form of methamphetamine, known as ice, is made by slow evaporation and recrystallization of methamphetamine as a hydrochloride salt, which results in large, clear crystals that can be smoked. Ice is considered to be both toxic and addictive.

Amphetamines can be made starting with precursor chemicals. A common method used phenyl-2-propanone (P2P) as the starting point until inclusion of this material on the list of controlled substances reduced its availability and forced clandestine labs to switch to other synthetic routes. The currently favored route starts with ephedrine, an ingredient in OTC antihistamine and cold medicines. Other ingredients in this synthetic route can include ammonia, sodium hydroxide (lye), and red phosphorus. Forensic chemists also help identify the synthesis method based on other materials present in the sample. In most cases it is possible to determine the material with which the drug has been diluted. Occasionally substances sold illegally as amphetamines are analyzed and found to contain nothing more than sugar and caffeine or ephedrine.

Oxycodone is a derivative of morphine that is used to relieve severe pain. It has been recently formulated as OxyContin, which is a time-released form. Oxycodone acts in the same manner as morphine and codeine, and like these substances, abuse can lead to physical and psychological addiction. OxyContin was introduced in 1995. Because the drug is time released, the amount of oxycodone in each tablet is much higher, and this has led to increasing abuse and diversion of OxyContin for illegal use. Abusers crush the tablets and by doing so destroy the time-releasing properties of the drug. This allows them to get a large dose immediately by ingestion, smoking, or injection with effects that mimic heroin. If whole tablets are available, forensic analysis of oxycodone and OxyContin consists of visual inspection and comparison of the tablets, with examples found in the *Physician's Desk Reference*.

Predator drugs, also called date rape drugs, render victims unconscious or otherwise unable to resist sexual assaults. Many drugs have been used in this way, most notably alcohol, but recently several other drugs have come to the attention of law enforcement. Of these two are currently of the most concern, Rohypnol and GHB. Rohypnol is the trade name for the drug flunitrazepam, which is not approved for use in the United States but is smuggled in from Europe and other areas. Rohypnol, also known as roofies, began to show up in the United States in the early 1990s in the form of a pill or crushed powder. It is tasteless and odorless and dissolves easily in liquids. As a result it is not difficult to slip the drug into a victim's drink and have it go undetected.

The drug can cause dizziness, confusion, nausea, blackouts, and loss of memory. The effects are intensified by alcohol and last eight to 24 hours. Traces of the drug can be detected in urine up to 72 hours after administration, although it is a difficult analysis. Detection is further complicated by the amnesia-inducing properties of the drug. Victims may not remember or may be unclear about the circumstances of the rape, resulting in delayed reporting or no reporting at all. In addition to its role in date rapes, Rohypnol is also abused in conjunction with other drugs such as heroin and cocaine, and long-term use can result in physical and psychological dependence.

A second date rape drug is gamma hydroxybutyrate (GHB), which was at one time used as a body-building supplement. It was pulled off health food store shelves in 1990. Easily synthesized, it has been abused in much the same way as Rohypnol. Low doses relieve tension and promote relaxation, but higher doses produces sleep (sometimes suddenly) and nausea, with alcohol enhancing these effects. Recognizing the dangers of GHB, regulators placed it on Schedule I of the CSA in 2000.

Lysergic acid diethylamine (LSD) is a potent hallucinogen that can be made from raw material extracted from natural sources or synthesized. Doses as low as 2 μg are sufficient to induce the drug's effects, which include alteration of sensory perceptions, hallucinations, a feeling of floating or being out of body, and extreme mood swings. Lysergic acid is a compound produced by a fungus that attacks grasses, a family that includes grains such as wheat and rye. Another precursor chemical, lysergic acid amide is found in the seeds of the morning glory flower.

Forensic chemists encounter many other types of drugs and evidence aside from the ones described above. Prescription drugs, odd white powders, unidentified plants, and a myriad other types of samples are submitted to forensic labs for analysis. When analytical chemistry is needed, it is the forensic chemists who are called on. For evidence suspected of containing drugs the role of the chemist is to determine if indeed an illegal substance is present and which one or ones they are. Other important determinations that the chemist typically makes are the weight of the evidence and, in some cases, the purity. When investigators need information about the source or trail that a drug has followed, the chemist may perform analyses as part of profiling. However, the role of the forensic chemist in most cases is simple: use modern techniques of analytical chemistry to identify any illegal drugs present in evidence.

5

Conclusions: The Future of Drugs, Poisons, and Chemistry

The world of forensic chemistry—illicit drugs and poisons in particular—never stands still. There will always be a race between those making and using illegal drugs and those working to detect, analyze, characterize, and control them. Illicit drugs go through cycles of birth, popularity, and decline. In the 1990s cocaine was a major concern; now it is methamphetamine. In 2020 it will be something else. What remains constant is the need for society to define what drugs it will control and for forensic chemistry to develop the analytical methods to analyze these drugs and poisons. Given this underlying reality, the future of forensic drug analysis and toxicology is very much tied to advances in analytical chemistry and the instruments used to conduct it.

Each year brings greater improvements in the capability, automation, and portability of chemical instrumentation. These advances trickle down to forensic chemistry and forensic biology, increasing throughput (number of samples that can be run in a day) and decreasing turnaround time. Soaring caseloads at laboratories often overwhelm these improvements. Yet, without these improvements crime laboratories would be quickly inundated. Autosamplers, which allow instruments to run unattended, have been a boon for drug analysis and toxicology, where much of the analysis requires instrumental data. Robotics systems are now capable of automating many of the tasks of sample preparation and transfer. While instruments and accessories cannot replace a forensic chemist, toxicologist, or biologist, automation maximizes the productivity of each, allowing the scientist to concentrate on analysis and interpretation.

New instrumentation and improved design of older instruments is also influencing forensic analysis. Much of this can be traced to decreasing costs as technologies mature. Many labs now use HPLC and HPLC–mass spectrometry (HPLC-MS), techniques that were rarely seen in forensic labs until the 1990s, both due to cost and method development considerations. HPLC-MS combines the separation power of high-performance liquid chromatography with the ability of mass spectrometry to identify definitively most molecules of interest to forensic chemists. The newest generation of HPLC-MS instruments actually consists of multiple mass spectrometers chained together, dramatically increasing the sensitivity and selectivity of the instrument. As a result forensic toxicologists may soon be able to detect many more drugs and metabolites at much lower concentrations than they could previously. This ability will be invaluable in many cases, such as when a person dies of subtle drug interactions or from poisoning by trace containments of clandestinely produced drugs.

A workhorse instrument in forensic chemistry, the IR spectrophotometer has seen advances in capability that will likely continue unabated. The driving force of much of this improvement lies with advancement in lasers and electronics. For inorganic analysis instruments such as the inductively coupled plasma mass spectrometer (ICP-MS) and inductively coupled plasma atomic emission spectroscope (ICP-AES) are expanding into forensic labs and will likely become commonplace in the next 10 to 20 years. These instruments allow for low-level detection of metals such as arsenic, chromium, and other potential poisons. Likewise, surface analysis instruments such as X-ray fluorescence (XRF) and scanning electron microscopes (SEM) are becoming affordable to more forensic labs, increasing capabilities and enlarging the scope of analyses available to the forensic examiner.

Finally, the world of genetics and forensic toxicology are starting to overlap, and the implications for forensic toxicology are likely to be significant. When a person takes a drug, enzymes are involved in the metabolism of that drug. Enzymes are proteins that are produced from genetic instructions encoded in that person's DNA. Many of the genes that code for enzymes are polymorphic, meaning that one person's version of the enzyme may be slightly different from another's. How these enzymes vary is inherited just as is eye color and blood type. The implication is that different people, because they have different versions of enzymes, will metabolize drugs and poisons differently. A person who efficiently metabolizes a drug could tolerate a higher dose than a person whose metabolism is less efficient. Thus, the lethal dose of drugs and drug combinations will vary. The study of genetic effects on drug metabolism is called pharmacogenetics, and it is likely to become an important aspect of forensic toxicology in the next 20 years.

GLOSSARY

adulterant   pharmacologically active material such as caffeine that is added to an illicit drug to dilute it

alkaloid   basic molecule obtained (or at one time obtained) from a plant. Alkaloids are basic due to the presence of an amine group. Caffeine, cocaine, and the opiates are examples of alkaloids.

anabolic steroid   steroid, natural or synthetic, that encourages muscle growth and purportedly improves athletic performance

analgesic   drug that alleviates pain, such as aspirin, acetaminophen, or morphine

anesthetic   substance that when administered to a person causes the person to enter a state of semiconsciousness or unconsciousness

barbiturate   family of drugs once widely used as sleeping aids. The introduction of benzodiazepines has reduced illicit use of barbiturates.

benzodiazepine   group of synthetic alkaloids used to treat anxiety, depression, and related ailments

biotransformation   chemical transformation of a substance that occurs within a biological system. Metabolism is a type of biotransformation.

Chemical Diversion and Trafficking Act (CDTA)   federal law passed in 1986 designed to limit access to precursor chemicals and pharmaceutical drugs used in clandestine synthesis

chromatography   process of separation of compounds in a mixture by means of selective partitioning between two phases. In gas chromatography compounds interact with a solid phase while gas flows through or over this solid phase. The compounds that interact more with the solid phase (i.e., partition selectively into it) will move slower than compounds that have greater affinity for the gas phase.

clandestine   secret or illegal. A clandestine laboratory is one that is used to make illegal drugs such as methamphetamine.

classification   the assigning an exhibit of evidence or other object to a group of like objects based on descriptors such as chemical and physical properties. Drugs, for example, can be classified as sedatives, hallucinogens, etc.

club drug   informal term describing drugs such as ecstasy (MDMA), GHB, LSD, and methamphetamine, used by people at clubs and parties

cocaine   alkaloid and central nervous system stimulant used medically as a topical anesthetic

codeine   opiate alkaloid found in the milky latex of opium poppies in concentrations of about 1–2 percent of the latex by weight.

colorimetry   form of spectroscopy in which information about a sample is obtained based on the color (wavelengths) of light that it absorbs

Controlled Substances Act (CSA)   federal law first passed in 1970 that places abused drugs on five schedules based on acceptable medical uses and potential for abuse

crystal test   presumptive test for drugs performed on a microscope slide. A reagent is added to a small sample, and the analyst studies any crystals that are formed using a microscope. Many drugs form crystals that are distinctive enough to aid in its identification.

cutting agent   substance used to dilute a drug. The substance can be pharmacologically active (adulterant, such as caffeine) or inactive (diluent, such as baking soda).

cystolithic hair   fine hairlike structure on the leaves of marijuana informally referred to as bear claw

date rape drug   *See* PREDATOR DRUG

depressant   class of drugs that causes depression of the central nervous system. Depressants cause slowed breathing and heart rate and sleepiness, among other symptoms. Alcohol is an example of a depressant

diluent   material added to dilute a drug. Unlike an adulterant, a diluent is pharmacologically inactive. Cornstarch and sugars are diluents.

drug   substance that is capable of inducing a physiological change when ingested. In contrast, a medicine is a combination of drugs.

Ecstasy street name for the stimulant MDMA, a predator drug and a club drug

entomotoxicology study of drugs, poisons, and their metabolites found in insects that have fed on a corpse. The goal of such analysis is to infer a possible cause of death for the person based on what is found in the insects.

ephedrine natural or semi-synthetic alkaloid that is used as a decongestant and a precursor in methamphetamine synthesis

exhibit piece or individual item of physical evidence

GHB gamma hydroxybutyric acid or gamma hydroxybutryate, a small acidic predator drug

gravimetric method older method of analytical chemistry in which the amount of a substance is determined through a weight. In other words, the detection system is a scale or analytical balance.

half-life amount of time for half of the original amount of a substance ingested or existing in the body to be eliminated or converted to another substance

hallucinogen drug that illicits a hallucination. LSD is an example of a hallucinogen.

hashish oily resin of the flowering tops of marijuana plants. Hashish has a high concentration of the active ingredient tetrahydrocannabinol.

heroin potent narcotic prepared by acetylation of morphine. It is also called diacetylmorphine and diamorphine.

human performance drug drug that alters human performance. The term is most often associated with sports, where athletes may take substances such as steroids to improve their athletic abilities.

immunoassay group of analytical methods that rely on antigen-antibody reactions to detect drugs or other target analytes

ingestion *See* MODE OF INGESTION

inhalant volatile substance that is abused by inhalation and that produces effects similar to anesthetics

intravenous into a vein, referring to a method of injection or drug delivery

ketamine veterinary anesthetic diverted for abuse as a dissociative anesthetic and club drug

LSD lysergic acid diethylamide, an ergot alkaloid and hallucinogen

lysergic acid   ergot alkaloid and precursor to LSD

MDMA   *See* ECSTASY

medicine   formulation that contains more than one drug. For example, liquid preparations used to alleviate the symptoms of a cold are medicines that contain mixtures of drugs such as aspirin, decongestants, and antihistamines.

mescaline   alkaloid obtained from the peyote cactus. Mescaline is an example of a hallucinogen.

metabolite   product of metabolic reaction and conversion

methamphetamine   synthetic alkaloid and central nervous system stimulant that is highly addictive

miscible   soluble. For example, table salt is miscible in water.

mode of ingestion   route or pathway by which a drug or poison enters the body. Common modes of ingestion are swallowing and injection

morphine   principal active opium alkaloid extracted from the opium poppy, found at approximately 10 percent levels in the milky latex

narcotic   class of drugs that relieves pain and encourages sleep. Morphine and heroin are narcotics.

natural drug or natural product   drug that is derived directly from a plant. Tetrahydrocannabinol and morphine are natural products.

NSAID   nonsteroidal anti-inflammatory drug, such as aspirin, that relieves pain by reducing inflammation at the site of injury

opiate alkaloid   alkaloid derived from the opium poppy. Codeine and heroin are examples of opiate alkaloids.

OxyContin   a time-released form of oxycodone that is widely abused. Users crush the tablets and take the entire dose at once.

pharmacodynamics   study of effects of drugs over time. Pharmacodynamics is concerned with the interaction of the drug with its target

pharmacokinetics   study of the movement of the drug and metabolic products through the body; typically divided into stages of absorption, distribution, metabolism, and elimination

pharmacology   study of how drugs behave once ingested. The field can be broadly divided into pharmacodynamics and pharmacokinetics.

postmortem toxicology   field that analyzes biological materials collected at autopsy

precursor   chemical compound, including pharmaceuticals that are used as the starting point for clandestine synthesis of controlled substances. A precursor can be immediate (one step from product) or distant (several steps).

predator drug   class of drugs used in date rape. These drugs render victims incapable of resisting unwanted sexual advances.

presumptive test   test used to narrow down the possible identity of a sample or to classify it. Results are not conclusive, and a positive result is best phrased as "more likely than not."

profiling   chemical analysis of substances found along with the drug of interest in a sample. The goal of profiling is to assist investigators in determining where a drug came from and how it was handled. Profiling analyses include stable isotope analysis and characterization of impurities found in the drug sample.

spectrophotometry or spectroscopy   class of analytical instrumental methods that are based on the interaction of electromagnetic energy with matter. Colorimetry is an example, in which visible light interacts with samples to reveal information about what is found in that sample.

spot test   another term for a color test or screening test used in drug analysis

stable isotope   isotope of an element that is found in stable ratios in nature. An isotope of an element is one that has the same number of protons in the nucleus but a different number of neutrons. Stable isotopes are useful for profiling.

steroid   class of compounds that act as hormones. The function of hormones is to transmit chemical messages within the body.

stimulant   class of drugs that stimulates the central nervous system resulting in elevated heart rate and less need for sleep. Methamphetamine is an example of a stimulant.

testosterone   male sex hormone that is produced in the testes. It plays a central role in the development of secondary sex characteristics. It is a steroid hormone derived from cholesterol.

tetrahydrocannabinol (THC)   principal active ingredient in marijuana; more completely called delta-9-tetrahydrocannabinol

thin-layer chromatography (TLC) form of chromatography in which the liquid phase is a solvent and the solid phase is a plate coated with a layer of material that can interact with compounds in the sample

tropane alkaloid alkaloid characterized by a bridged structure across a ring. Cocaine is a tropane alkaloid.

FURTHER READING

Print Sources
Analytical and Forensic Chemistry

Bell, S. C. *Forensic Chemistry.* Upper Saddle River, N.J.: Pearson/Prentice Hall, 2006. This is a general textbook covering forensic drug analysis, forensic toxicology, and forensic chemistry.

Buffington, R., and M. K. Wilson. *Detectors for Gas Chromatography: A Practical Primer.* Avondale, Pa.: HewlettPackard, 1987. A primer on the common types of detectors used in gas chromatography.

Dean, J. A. *Analytical Chemistry Handbook.* New York: McGraw Hill, 1995. A reference book containing information about many chemical methods and techniques.

Eiceman, G. A., and Z. Karpus. *Ion Mobility Spectrometry.* Boca Raton, Fla.: CRC Press, 1995. A definitive summary of the principles and theory of ion mobility spectrometry.

Fritz, J. S. *Analytical Solid Phase Extraction.* New York: Wiley VCH, 1999. A handbook describing the theory and practice of common solid-phase extraction methods.

Harris, D. C. *Quantitative Chemical Analysis.* 4th ed. New York: W. H. Freeman, 1995. A widely used college textbook that covers the fundamentals of analytical chemistry including gravimetric methods.

Jenkins, R. *X-ray Fluorescence Spectrometry.* Chemical Analysis: A Series of Monographs on Analytical Chemistry and Its Applications. New York: John Wiley & Sons, 1988. An overview of this instrumental technique.

Skoog, D. A., et al., *Analytical Chemistry, an Introduction.* 7th ed. Orlando, Fla.: Harcourt College Publishers, 2000. A good summary of the common types of instrumental methods of analysis.

Yinon, J., ed. *Forensic Applications of Mass Spectrometry.* Boca Raton, Fla.: CRC Press, 1995. An older but still useful summary of how mass spectrometry is used in forensic science and forensic chemistry.

General References

The following resources address forensic science topics such as laws of evidence, forensic drug analysis, and forensic chemistry.

Introductory Level

De Forest, P. R., R. E. Gaensslen, and H. C. Lee. *Forensic Science: An Introduction to Criminalistics.* New York: McGraw Hill, 1983.

Eckert, W. E., ed. *Introduction to Forensic Sciences.* 2d ed. Boca Raton, Fla.: CRC Press, 1992.

James, S. H., and J. J. Nordby, eds. *Forensic Science: An Introduction to Scientific and Investigative Techniques.* 2d ed. Boca Raton, Fla.: CRC Press, 2006.

Nickell, J. N., and J. F. Fisher. *Crime Science: Methods of Forensic Detection.* Lexington: University Press of Kentucky, 1998.

Nordby, J. J. *Dead Reckoning: The Art of Forensic Detection.* Boca Raton, Fla.: CRC Press, 2000.

Law

Becker, R. F. *Scientific Evidence and Expert Testimony Handbook.* Springfield, Ill.: Charles C. Thomas, 1997.

Black's Law Dictionary. 6th ed. St. Paul, Minn.: West Publishing Company, 1990.

Moenssens, A. A., et al. *Scientific Evidence in Civil and Criminal Cases.* 4th ed. Westbury, N.Y.: Foundation Press, 1995.

Toxicology

Levine, B. *Principles of Forensic Toxicology.* Washington, D.C.: American Association of Clinical Chemistry, 1999.

Web Sources
Drugs in Sports/Sports Toxicology

United States Anti-Doping Agency. *2008 Guide to Prohibited Substances and Prohibited Methods of Doping.* Available online. URL: http://www.usantidoping.org/files/active/what/usada_guide.pdf. Downloaded January 8, 2008. Lists banned substances.

United States Olympic Committee Anti-Doping Agency. Available online. URL: http://www.usoc.org/12696.htm. Downloaded January 2, 2008. A description of the role; function, and structure of this agency.

United States Olympic Committee National Anti-Doping Policies. Available online. URL: http://www.usolympicteam.com/National_Anti-Doping_Poliicies_August_13_04.pdf. Downloaded January 2, 2008. Policies that apply to U.S. athletes.

World Anti-Doping Association. Available online. URL: http://www.wada-ama.org/en. Accessed December 18, 2007. Description of the organization and its function.

General

American Association of Poison Control Centers. *AAPCC Annual Data Report: 2005 Annual Report of the American Association of Poison Control Centers' National Poisoning and Exposure Data.* Available online. URL: http://www.aapcc.org/Annual%20Reports/05report/2005%20Published.pdf. Downloaded December 15, 2007. Statistics on poisonings in the United States.

National Highway Traffic Safety Administration. Available online. URL: http://www.nhtsa.dot.gov. Downloaded January 2, 2008. Data on traffic accidents including alcohol-related.

———. *National Survey of Drinking and Driving Attitudes and Behavior.* Available online. URL: http://www.nhtsa.dot.gov/staticfiles/DOT/NHTSA/Traffic%20Injury%20Control/Articles/Associated%20Files/DD2001v1.pdf. Downloaded January 2, 2008. Current survey results and data.

Nikon's Microscopy University. Available online. URL: http://www. microscopyu.com. Accessed December 17, 2007. A Web site designed to provide an educational forum for all aspects of optical microscopy, digital imaging, and photomicrography.

Reddy's Forensic Page. Available online. URL: http://www.forensicpage. com. Accessed January 2, 2008. A collection of forensic links.

United States Department of Labor, Occupational Safety and Health Administration. "Hazard Information Bulletin 19980309." Available online. URL: http://www.osha.gov/dts/hib/hib_data/hib19980309. html. Downloaded December 29, 2007. Information about workplace issues related to exposures.

Zeno's Forensic Page. Available online. URL: http://www.forensic.to/ forensic.html. Accessed January 2, 2008. A collection of forensic links.

Professional Organizations and Societies

American Academy of Forensic Sciences (AAFS). 410 North 21st Street, Colorado Springs, CO 80904. Tel.: (719) 636-1100. URL: http://www. aafs.org. Includes several Divisions of forensic science.

American Board of Criminalistics (ABC). PO Box 1123, Wausau, WI 54402-1123. URL: http://www.criminalistics.com. The organization that coordinates certification of many forensic science specialties and practitioners.

American Board of Forensic Toxicology (ABFT). 410 North 21st Street, Colorado Springs, CO 80904. Tel.: (719) 636-1100. URL: http://www. abft.org. A professional toxicology board.

American Board of Medicolegal Death Investigators (ABMDI). 1402 South Grand Boulevard, St. Louis, MO 63104-1028. Tel.: (314) 977-5970. URL: http://www.slu.edu/organizations/abmdi. Organization of death investigators.

American Chemical Society (ACS). 1155 16th Street NW, Washington, DC 20036. Tel.: (800) 227-5558. URL: http://www.chemistry.org. The largest scientific society in the world.

American Society for Testing Materials (ASTM). 100 Barr Harbor Drive, PO Box C700, West Conshohocken, PA 19428-2959. Tel.:

(800) 262-1373. URL: http://www.astm.org. A group dedicated to standardization.

American Society of Crime Laboratory Directors (ASCLD). 139K Technology Drive, Garner, NC 27529. Tel.: (919) 773-2044. URL: http://www.ascld.org. A group that includes laboratory directors and that is active in laboratory accreditation.

Society for Forensic Toxicologists (SOFT). One MacDonald Center, 1 North MacDonald Street, Suite 15, Mesa, AZ 85201. Tel.: (888) 866-SOFT (7638). URL: http://www.softtox.org. A professional association of forensic toxicologists.

Periodic Table of the Elements

Key:

3 Li 6.941

3 — Atomic number
Li — Symbol
6.941 — Atomic weight

1 IA	2 IIA		3 IIIB	4 IVB	5 VB	6 VIB	7 VIIB	8 VIIIB	9 VIIIB	10 VIIIB	11 IB	12 IIB	13 IIIA	14 IVA	15 VA	16 VIA	17 VIIA	18 VIIIA
1 H 1.00794																		2 He 4.0026
3 Li 6.941	4 Be 9.0122												5 B 10.81	6 C 12.011	7 N 14.0067	8 O 15.9994	9 F 18.9984	10 Ne 20.1798
11 Na 22.9898	12 Mg 24.3051												13 Al 26.9815	14 Si 28.0855	15 P 30.9738	16 S 32.067	17 Cl 35.4528	18 Ar 39.948
19 K 39.0938	20 Ca 40.078		21 Sc 44.9559	22 Ti 47.867	23 V 50.9415	24 Cr 51.9962	25 Mn 54.938	26 Fe 55.845	27 Co 58.9332	28 Ni 58.6934	29 Cu 63.546	30 Zn 65.409	31 Ga 69.723	32 Ge 72.61	33 As 74.9216	34 Se 78.96	35 Br 79.904	36 Kr 83.798
37 Rb 85.4678	38 Sr 87.62		39 Y 88.906	40 Zr 91.224	41 Nb 92.9064	42 Mo 95.94	43 Tc (98)	44 Ru 101.07	45 Rh 102.9055	46 Pd 106.42	47 Ag 107.8682	48 Cd 112.412	49 In 114.818	50 Sn 118.711	51 Sb 121.760	52 Te 127.60	53 I 126.9045	54 Xe 131.29
55 Cs 132.9054	56 Ba 137.328	57-70 ☆	71 Lu 174.967	72 Hf 178.49	73 Ta 180.948	74 W 183.84	75 Re 186.207	76 Os 190.23	77 Ir 192.217	78 Pt 195.08	79 Au 196.9655	80 Hg 200.59	81 Tl 204.3833	82 Pb 207.2	83 Bi 208.9804	84 Po (209)	85 At (210)	86 Rn (222)
87 Fr (223)	88 Ra (226)	89-102 ★	103 Lr (260)	104 Rf (261)	105 Db (262)	106 Sg (266)	107 Bh (262)	108 Hs (263)	109 Mt (268)	110 Ds (271)	111 Rg (272)	112 Uub (277)	113 Uut (284)	114 Uuq (285)	115 Uup (288)	116 Uuh (292)	117 Uus ?	118 Uuo ?

Numbers in parentheses are atomic mass numbers of most stable isotopes.

☆ Lanthanoids	57 La 138.9055	58 Ce 140.115	59 Pr 140.908	60 Nd 144.24	61 Pm (145)	62 Sm 150.36	63 Eu 151.966	64 Gd 157.25	65 Tb 158.9253	66 Dy 162.500	67 Ho 164.9303	68 Er 167.26	69 Tm 168.9342	70 Yb 173.04
★ Actinoids	89 Ac (227)	90 Th 232.0381	91 Pa 231.036	92 U 238.0289	93 Np (237)	94 Pu (244)	95 Am 243	96 Cm (247)	97 Bk (247)	98 Cf (251)	99 Es (252)	100 Fm (257)	101 Md (258)	102 No (259)

© Infobase Publishing

The Chemical Elements

(g) none (c) nonmetallics

element	symbol	a.n.
carbon	C	6
hydrogen	H	1

(g) chalcogen (c) nonmetallics

element	symbol	a.n.
oxygen	O	8
polonium	Po	84
selenium	Se	34
sulfur	S	16
tellurium	Te	52
ununhexium	Uuh	116

(g) alkali metal (c) metallics

element	symbol	a.n.
cesium	Cs	55
francium	Fr	87
lithium	Li	3
potassium	K	19
rubidium	Rb	37
sodium	Na	11

(g) alkaline earth metal (c) metallics

element	symbol	a.n.
barium	Ba	56
beryllium	Be	4
calcium	Ca	20
magnesium	Mg	12
radium	Ra	88
strontium	Sr	38

(g) none (c) metallics

element	symbol	a.n.
aluminum	Al	13
bohrium	Bh	107
cadmium	Cd	48
chromium	Cr	24
cobalt	Co	27
copper	Cu**	29
darmstadium	Ds	110
dubnium	Db	105
gallium	Ga	31
gold	Au***	79
hafnium	Hf	72
hassium	Hs	108
indium	In	49
iridium	Ir****	77
iron	Fe	26
lawrencium	Lr	103
lead	Pb	82
lutetium	Lu	71
manganese	Mn	25
meitnerium	Mt	109
mercury	Hg	80
molybdenum	Mo	42
nickel	Ni	28
niobium	Nb	41
osmium	Os****	76
palladium	Pd****	46
platinum	Pt****	78
rhenium	Re	75
rhodium	Rh****	45
roentgenium	Rg	111
ruthenium	Ru****	44
rutherfordium	Rf	104

element	symbol	a.n.
scandium	Sc	21
seaborgium	Sg	106
silver	Ag***	47
tantalum	Ta	73
technetium	Tc	43
thallium	Tl	81
titanium	Ti	22
tin	Sn	50
tungsten	W	74
ununbium	Uub	112
ununtrium	Uut	113
ununquadium	Uuq	114
vanadium	V	23
yttrium	Y	39
zinc	Zn	30
zirconium	Zr	40

(g) pnictogen (c) metallics

element	symbol	a.n.
arsenic	As*	33
antimony	Sb*	51
bismuth	Bi	83
nitrogen	N	7
phosophorus	P**	15
ununpentium	Uup	115

(g) none (c) semimetallics

element	symbol	a.n.
boron	B	5
germanium	Ge	32
silicon	Si	14

(g) actinoid (c) metallics

element	symbol	a.n.
actinium	Ac	89
americium	Am	95
berkelium	Bk	97
californium	Cf	98
curium	Cm	96
einsteinium	Es	99
fermium	Fm	100
mendelevium	Md	101
neptunium	Np	93
nobelium	No	102
plutonium	Pu	94
protactinium	Pa	91
thorium	Th	90
uranium	U	92

(g) halogens (c) nonmetallics

element	symbol	a.n.
astatine	At*	85
bromine	Br*	35
chlorine	Cl	17
fluorine	F	9
iodine	I	53
ununseptium	Uus*	117

(g) lanthanoid (c) metallics

element	symbol	a.n.
cerium	Ce	58
dysprosium	Dy	66
erbium	Er	68
europium	Eu	63
gadolinium	Gd	64
holmium	Ho	67
lanthanum	La	57
neodymium	Nd	60
praseodymium	Pr	59
promethium	Pm	61
samarium	Sm	62
terbium	Tb	65
thulium	Tm	69
ytterbium	Yb	70

(g) noble gases (c) nonmetallics

element	symbol	a.n.
argon	Ar	18
helium	He	2
krypton	Kr	36
neon	Ne	10
radon	Rn	86
xenon	Xe	54
ununoctium	Uuo	118

* = semimetallics (c)
** = nonmetallics (c)
*** = coinage metal (g)
**** = precious metal (g)

a.n. = atomic number
(g) = group
(c) = classification

© Infobase Publishing

INDEX

Italic page numbers indicate illustrations.